Kelowna British Columbia Canada in Colour Photos, Saving Our History One Photo at a Time

Photography
by Barbara Raué
©2018

Series Name:
Cruising Canada

Book 12: Kelowna B.C.

Cover photo: 1912 Abbott Street, Page 57

Series Name: Cruising Canada
Saving Our History One Photo at a Time in colour photos

Book 1-9: Winnipeg Manitoba
Book 10: Osoyoos, B.C.
Book 11: Vernon, Salmon Arm
Book 12: Kelowna

Other Books by Barbara Raue

Coins of Gold
Arrows, Indians and Love
The Life and Times of Barbara
The Cromwell Family Book
Laura Secord Discovered
Daddy Where Are You?

Montana Series
Book 1: Montana Dream
Book 2: Life on the Montana Frontier
Book 3: Montana to Boston and Back
Book 4: Montana Sons Go to War
Book 5: Montana Sons Return From War

Visit Barbara's website to view all of my books
http://barbararaue.ca

© 2018 by Barbara Raue - All the photos in this book have been taken with my cameras. I own the rights to them.

The Kelowna town site was laid out in 1892, and by 1898 the community growing on the shores of Okanagan Lake began to show that it would become a permanent settlement. As people came so did the travelling missionaries and students of both the Presbyterian and Methodist churches. Kelowna is the largest community in the Okanagan Valley.

The Okanagan Sunflower is the official floral emblem of Kelowna. It is one of the longest blooming wildflowers, providing abundant splashes of bright yellow on the hillsides in early spring. The plant is drought tolerant; it's completely edible and was used by the First Nations peoples as a food source. Its large yellow flowers reflect the sunny Okanagan skies and the hot summer climate.

The service industry employs the most people in Kelowna. In summer, boating, swimming, waterskiing, windsurfing, fishing, golfing, hiking and biking are popular. In winter both Alpine and Nordic skiing are favorite activities at the nearby ski resorts. Kelowna produces wines that have received international recognition. Vineyards are found around and south of the city where the climate is ideal for the many wineries. Kelowna is the home of Sun-Rype, a popular manufacturer of fruit bars and juices.

Many prominent people played a part in Kelowna becoming the city it is today and many of them made their homes on Marshall Street. The W.J. Marshall family was one of the very early families to settle here and their home is at 1869. R.B. Staples owned the Beaverdell Silver Mine and was also prominent in the fruit industry; their home is at 1812.

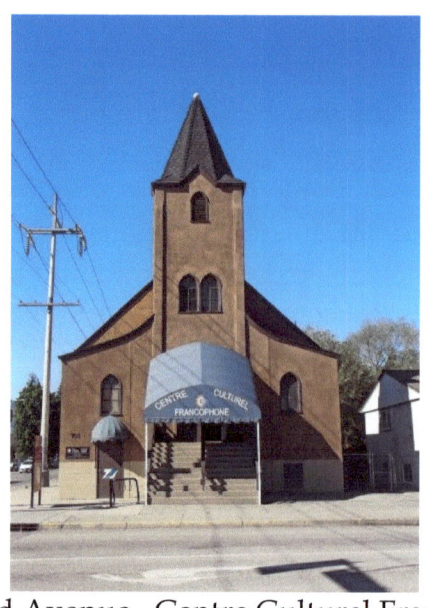

702 Bernard Avenue –Centre Culturel Francophone – Lutheran Church built 1949 – Gothic Revival with symmetrical design and central steeple

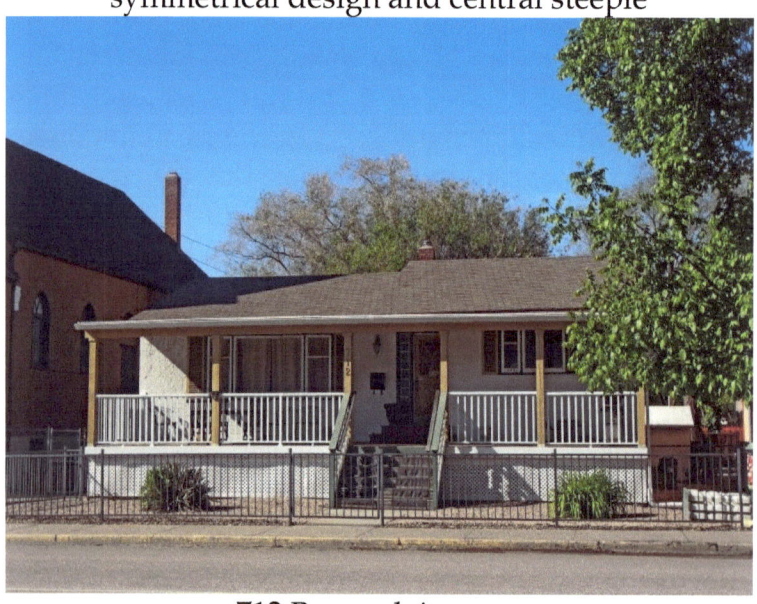

712 Bernard Avenue

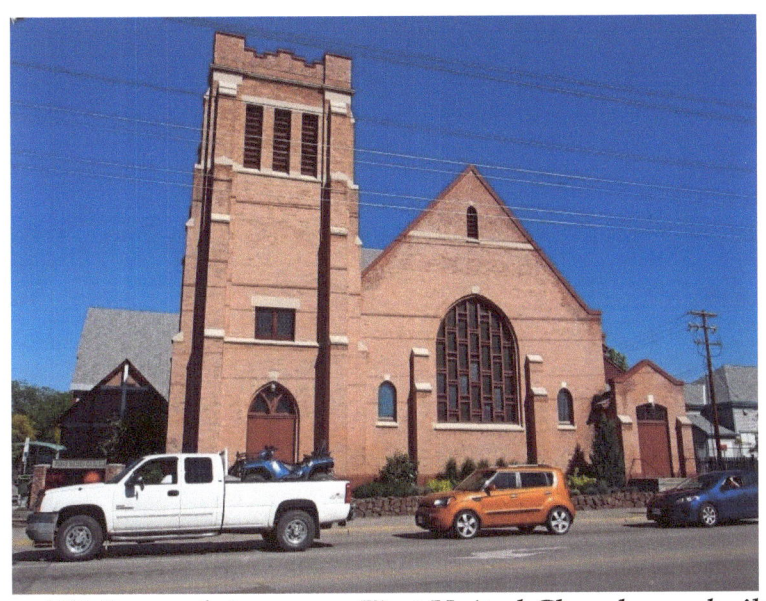

721 Bernard Avenue – First United Church was built in 1909 of locally kilned brick in the late Gothic Revival Style. The building sits in a prominent position at the intersection of Bernard Avenue and Richter Street. It has an asymmetrical plan, with a corner entry through the base of the tower. The Gothic Revival features include pointed-arched and segmental-headed doors, pointed-arched stained-glass windows, buttresses that are stepped with sloped coping at each step, gables, and a crenellated tower. Light brown brick church walls have cream concrete trim. Large stained-glass windows dominate the two main church facades.

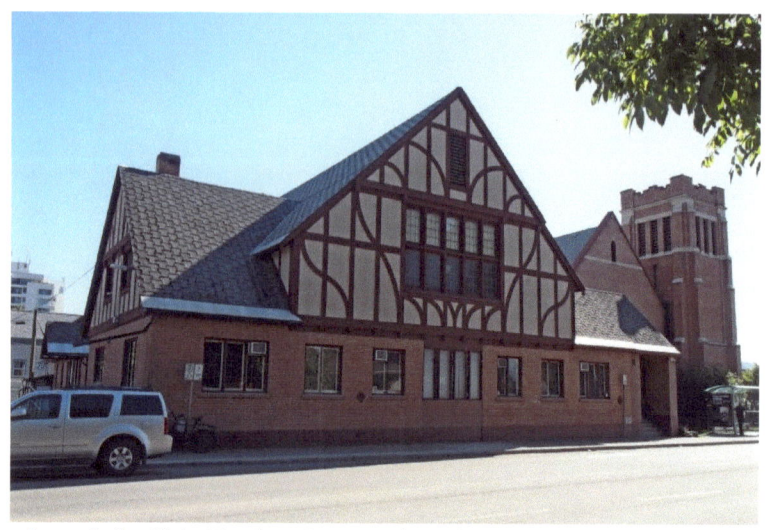
The church hall is Tudor Revival style and was added in 1929.

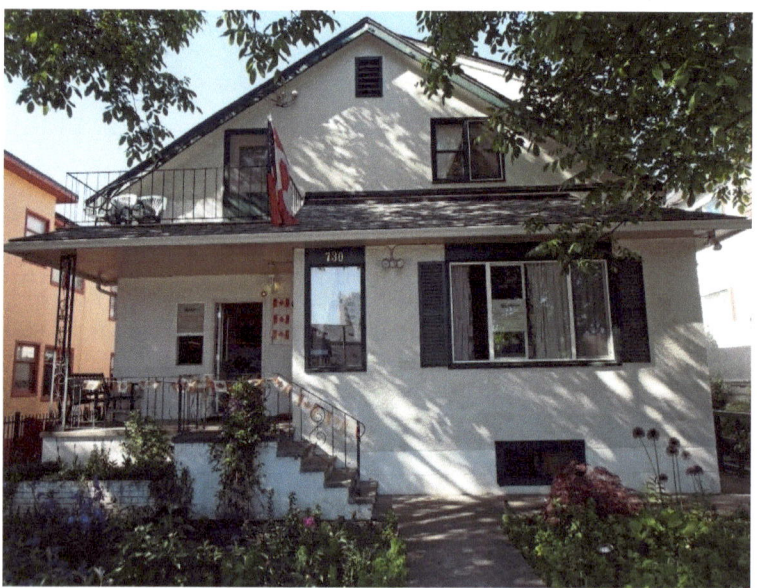
730 Bernard Avenue

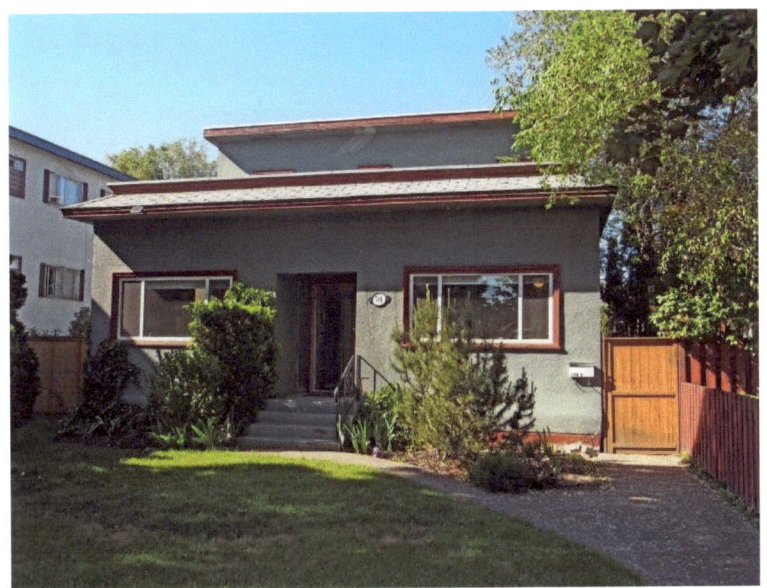

748 Bernard Avenue

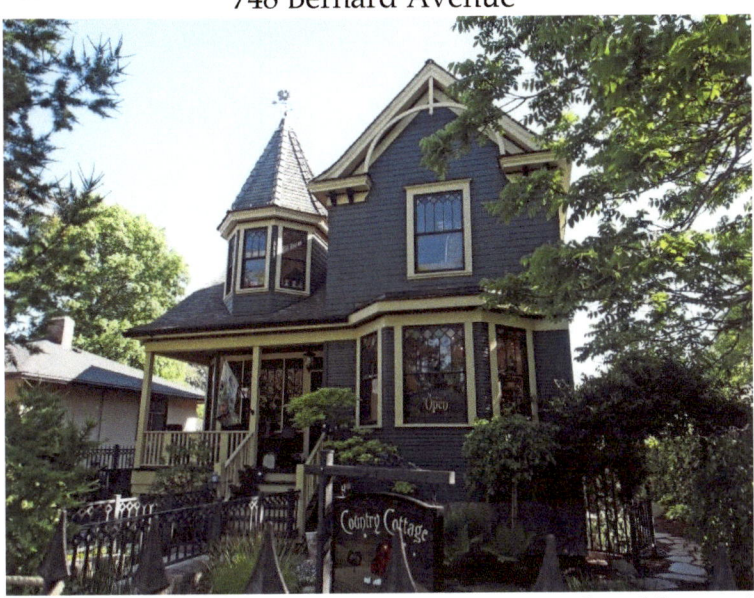

763 Bernard Avenue – 1910 - W.F. Muirhead house is in the Queen Anne style which is characterized by its asymmetrical composition, vertical proportions, octagonal tower, bay window and flaring "belcast" eaves. There is a decorative wood arch on the gable.

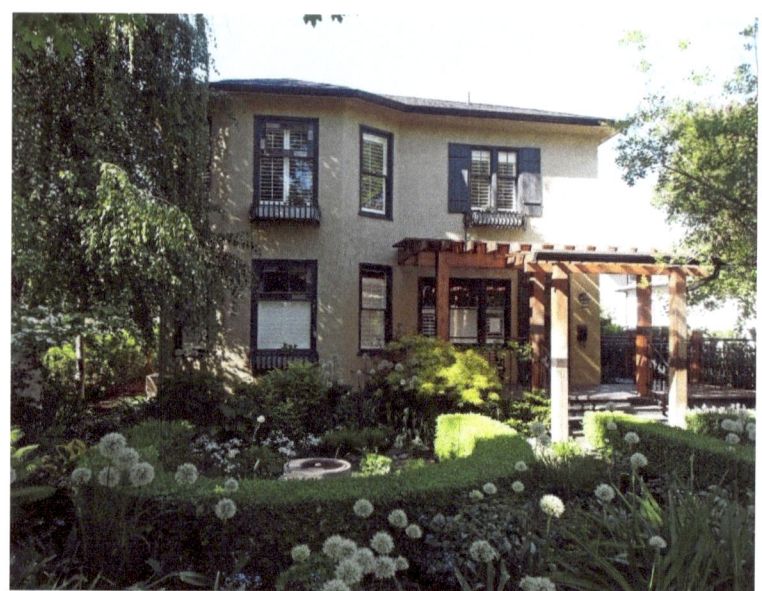

770 Bernard Avenue – 1907 – Frank DeHart (Mayor) House – hipped roof, foursquare design with Arts and Crafts elements, two-storey bay window

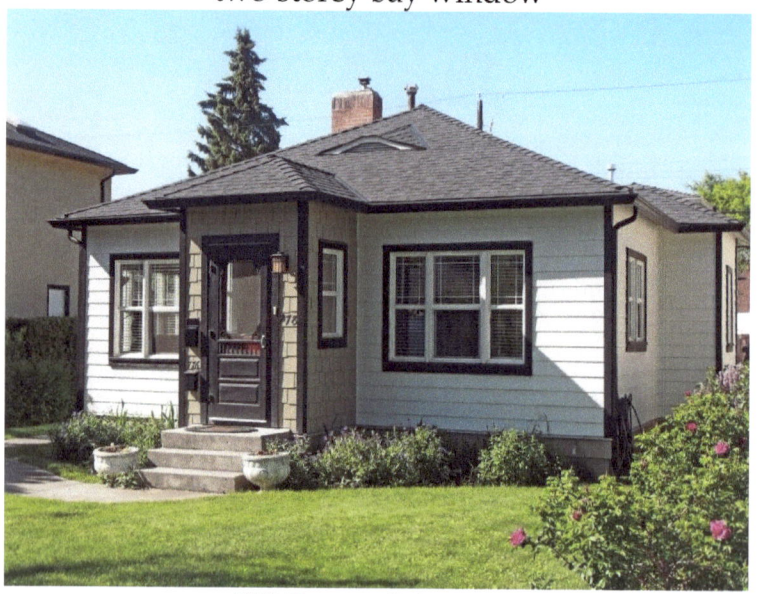

778 Bernard Avenue

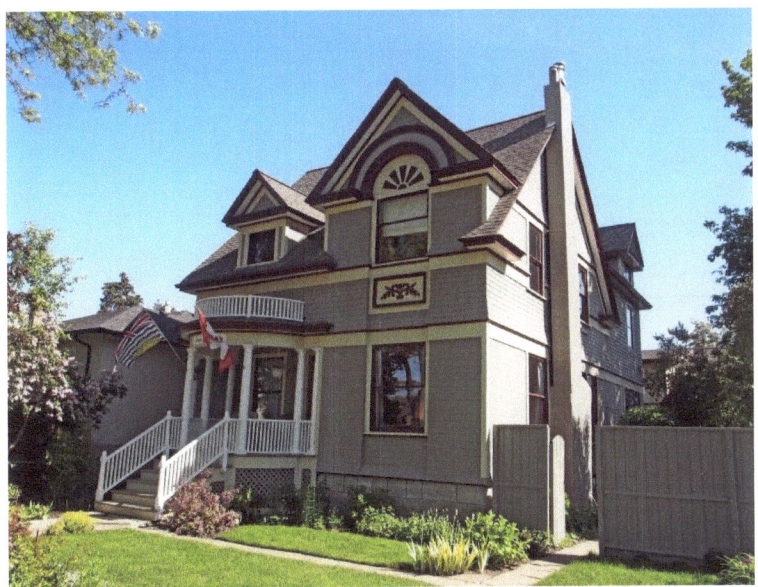

781 Bernard Avenue – The David Leckie (successful businessman and civic leader) House was built in 1906 in the late Queen Anne style. A tall gable on the right is balanced by a dormer on the left. There is narrow horizontal wood siding and a semi-circular porch with a balustrade above.

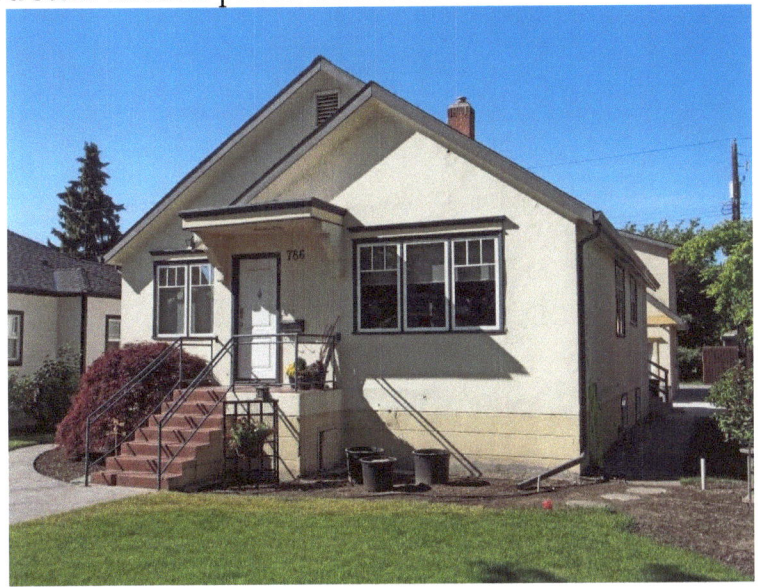

786 Bernard Avenue

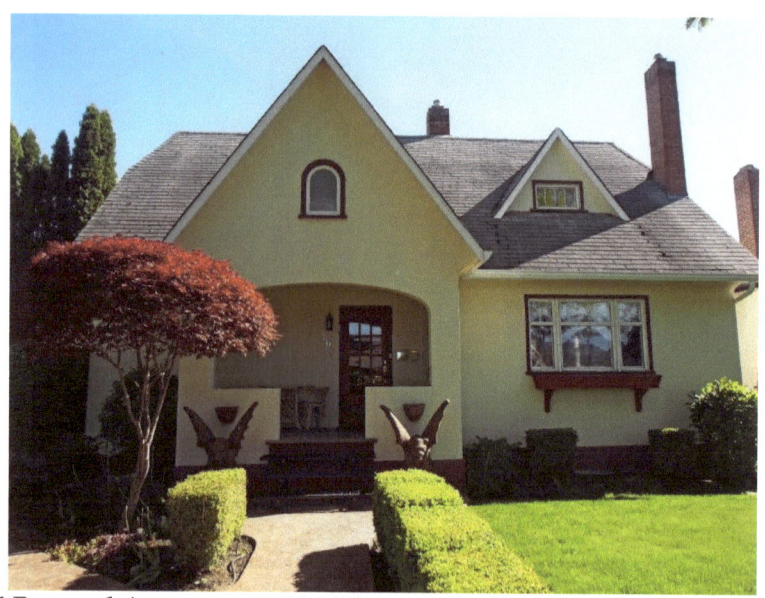

795 Bernard Avenue – 1936 – Thomas Ryall House Arts and Crafts cottage with steep gables

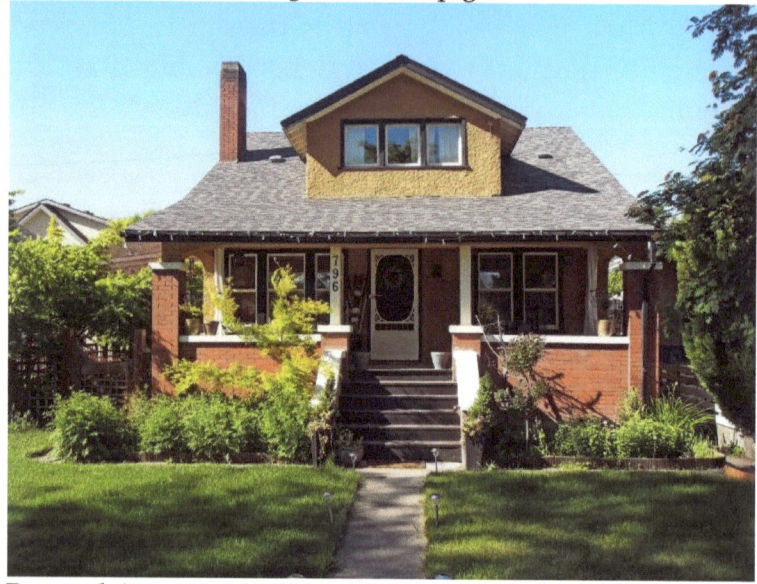

796 Bernard Avenue – William Harvey (accountant) House – 1926 – Craftsman Bungalow style with a flaring gable roof, dormer, broad eaves, deep brick front porch

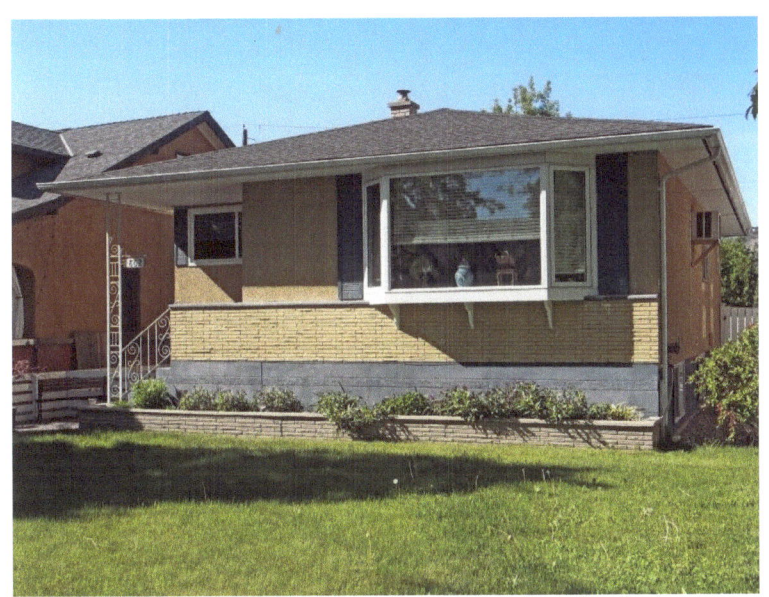

802 Bernard Avenue

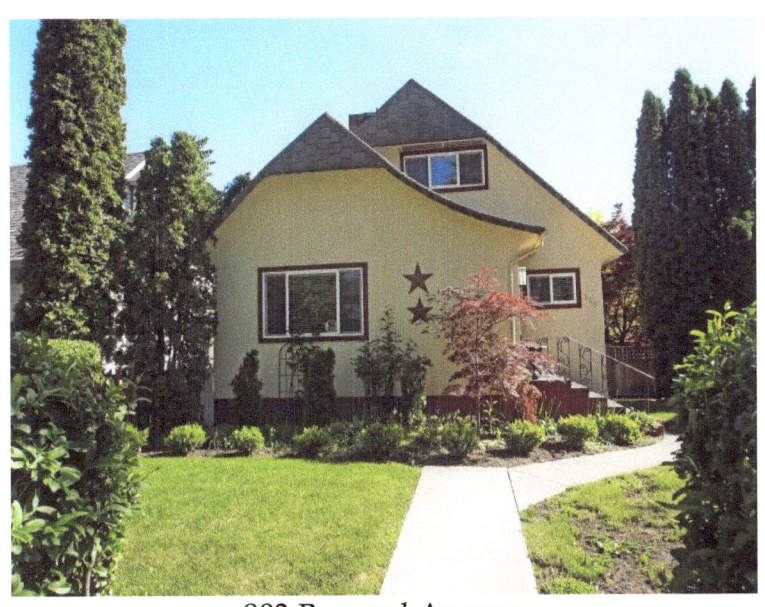

803 Bernard Avenue

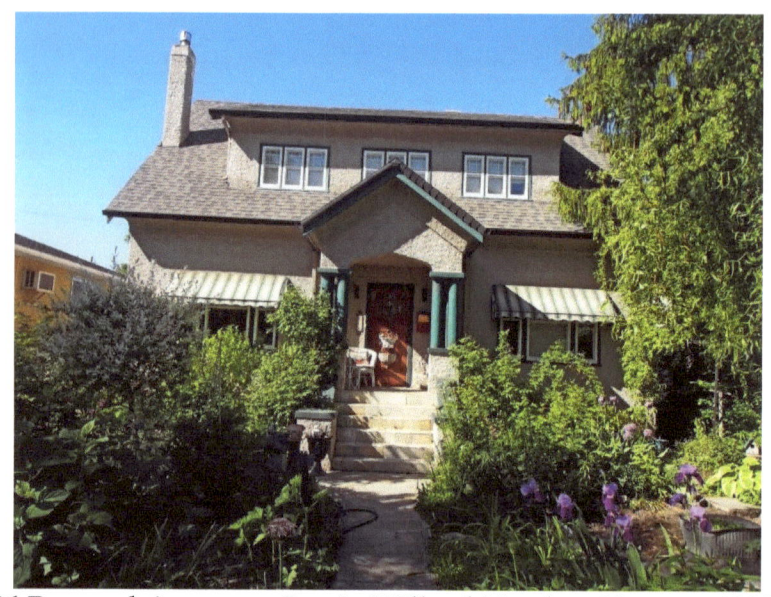

806 Bernard Avenue – Jessie Willard Hughes House - 1933 – Colonial Revival style – JW Hughes planted the first commercial vineyards in 1926 and he exported gladioli and peony bulbs.

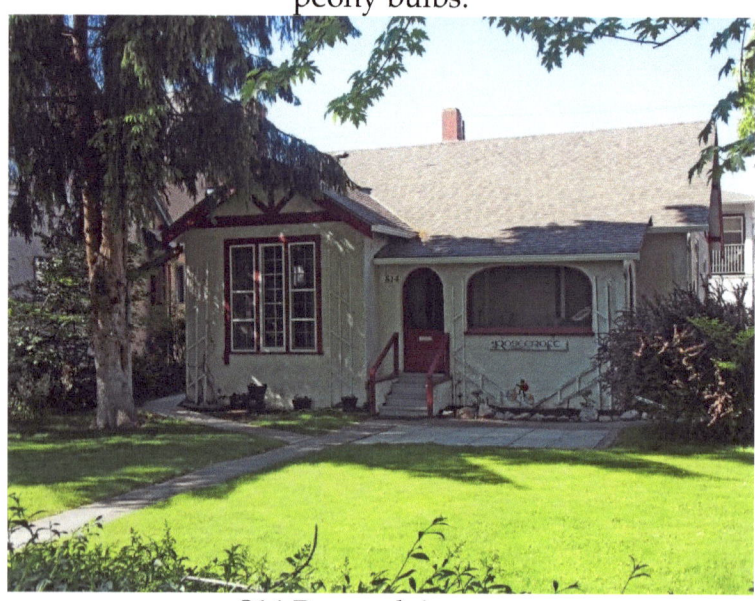

814 Bernard Avenue

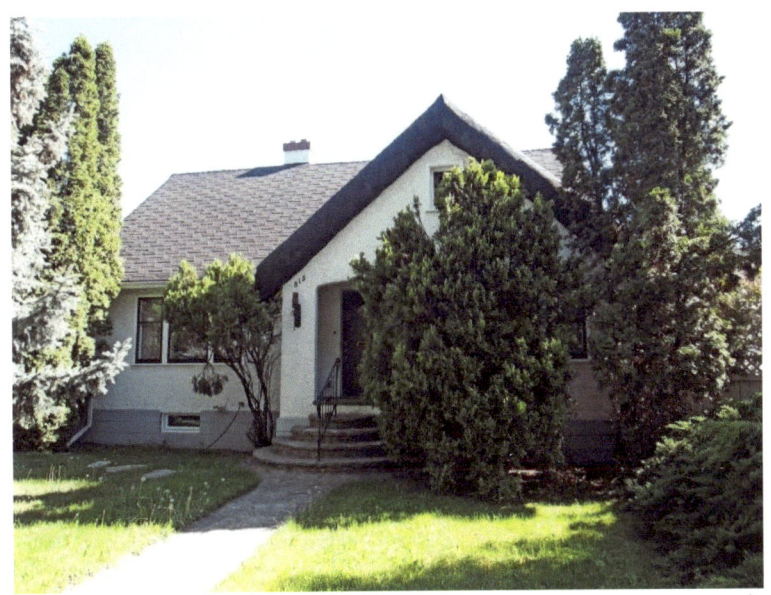

815 Bernard Avenue – Winter House – 1939 – Vernacular Cottage

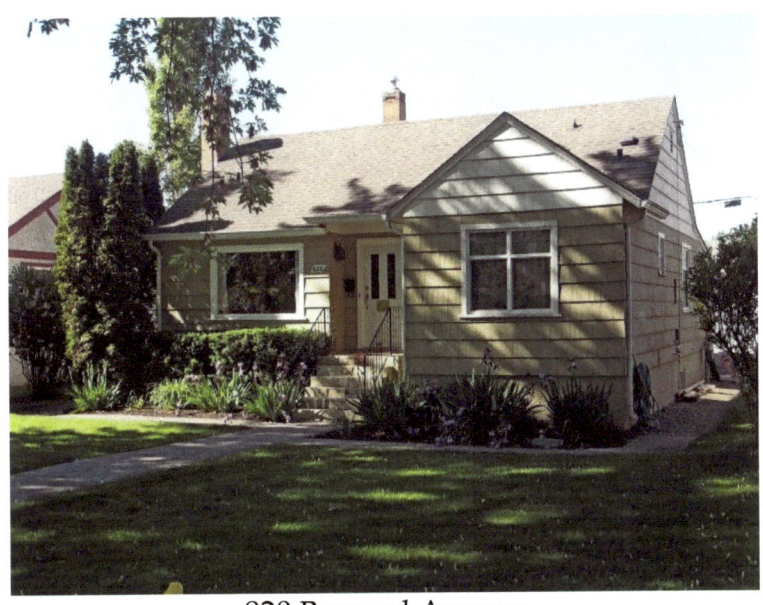

820 Bernard Avenue

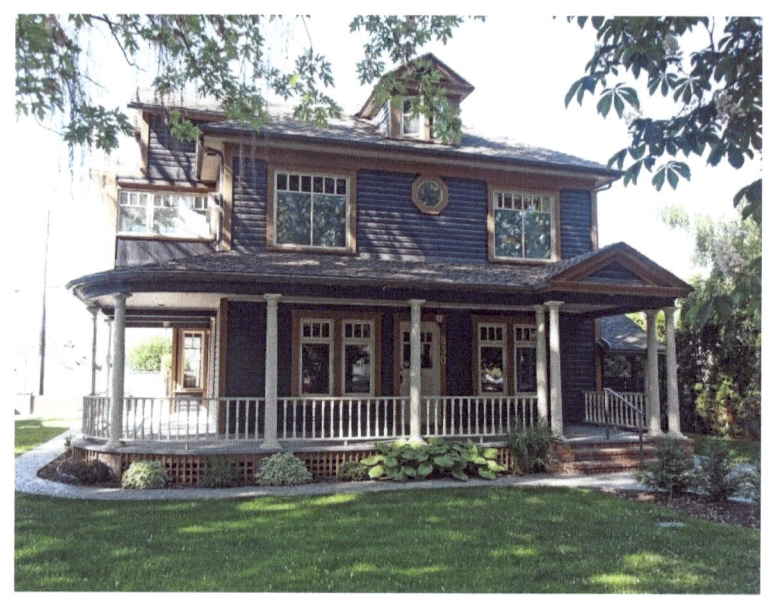

830 Bernard Avenue – James W. Jones (Mayor, Conservative MLA) – 1912 – Queen Anne style, hipped roof with dormer, classic foursquare, wraparound pillared veranda, narrow horizontal wood siding

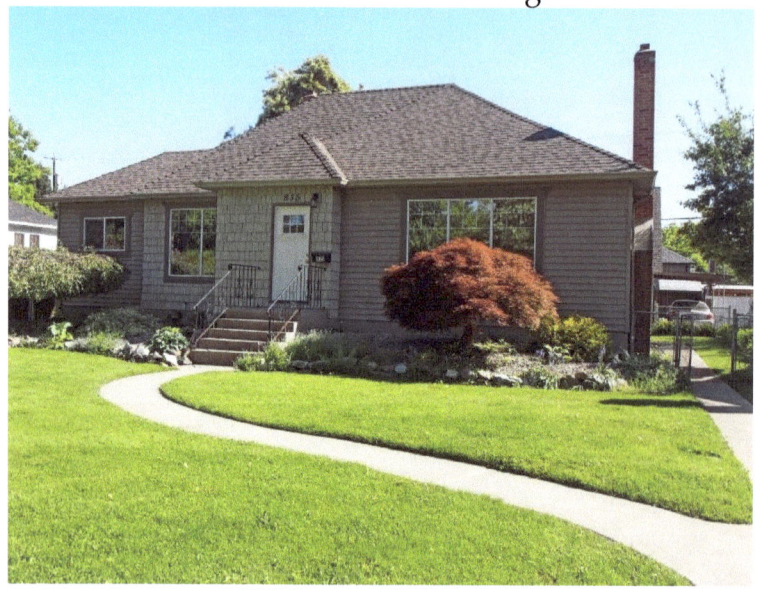

835 Bernard Avenue

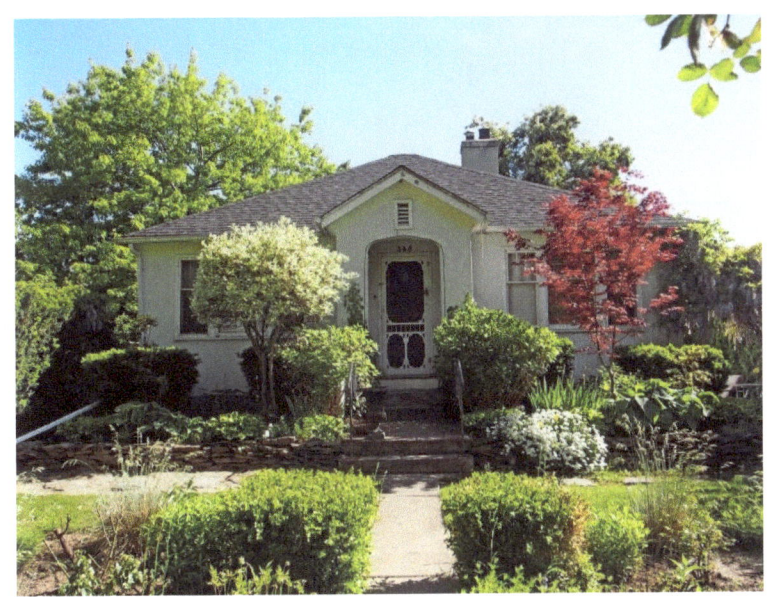

845 Bernard Avenue

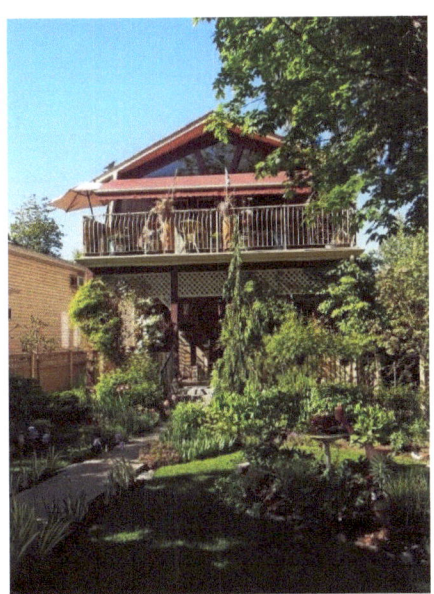

848 Bernard Avenue

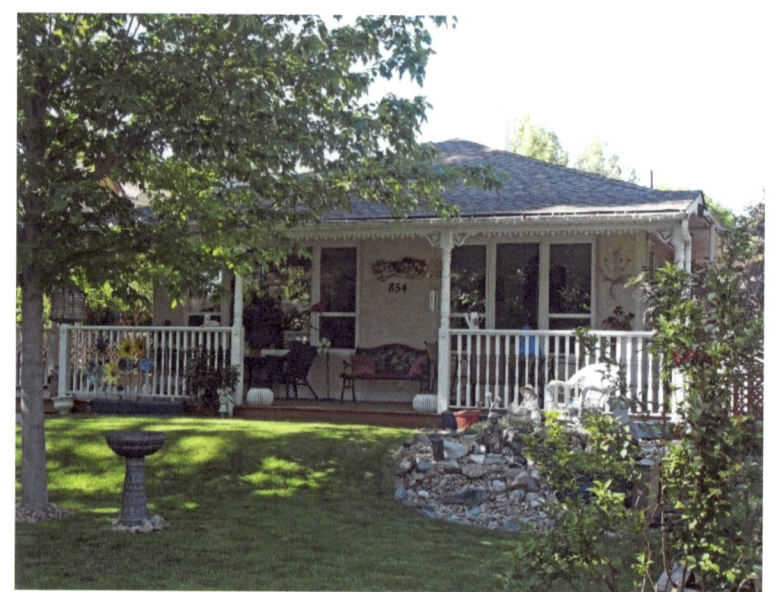

854 Bernard Avenue

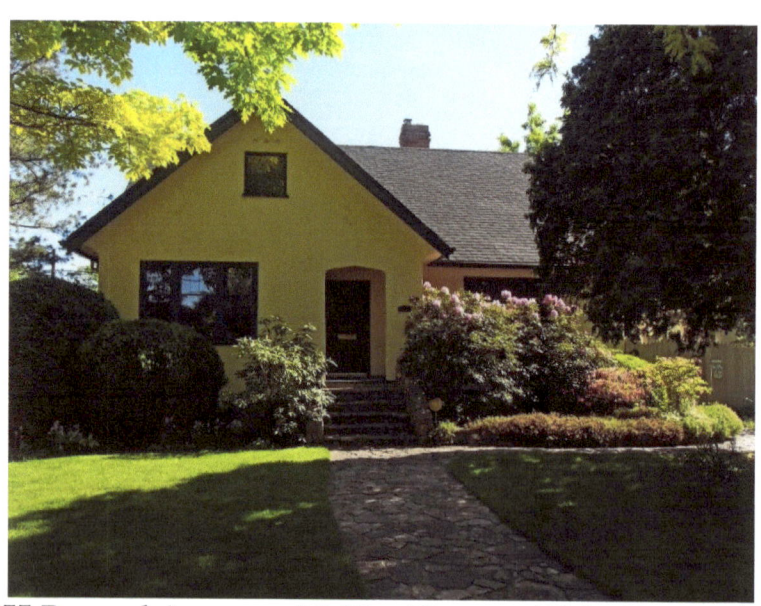

855 Bernard Avenue – McKim House – 1936 – Vernacular cottage with a cross-gable roof

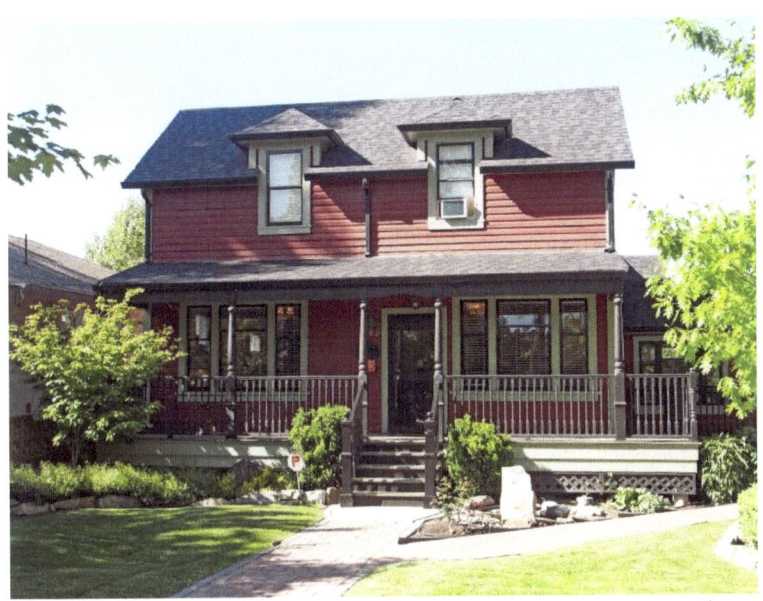

862 Bernard Avenue – 1905 – Cooper House - Vernacular style – 1½-storey height with gabled roof

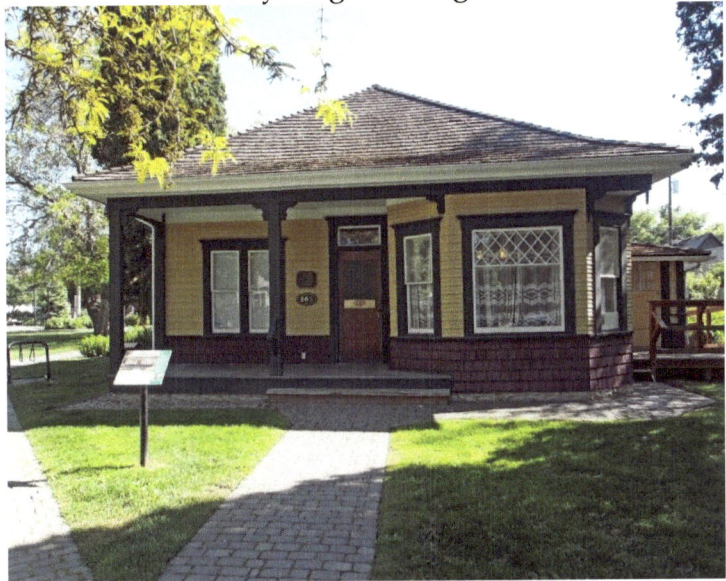

865 Bernard Avenue – James Bacon Knowles (jeweller and watch maker) house built in 1907 – hipped roof, wood frame construction with double-bevelled wooden siding, wooden trim and details.

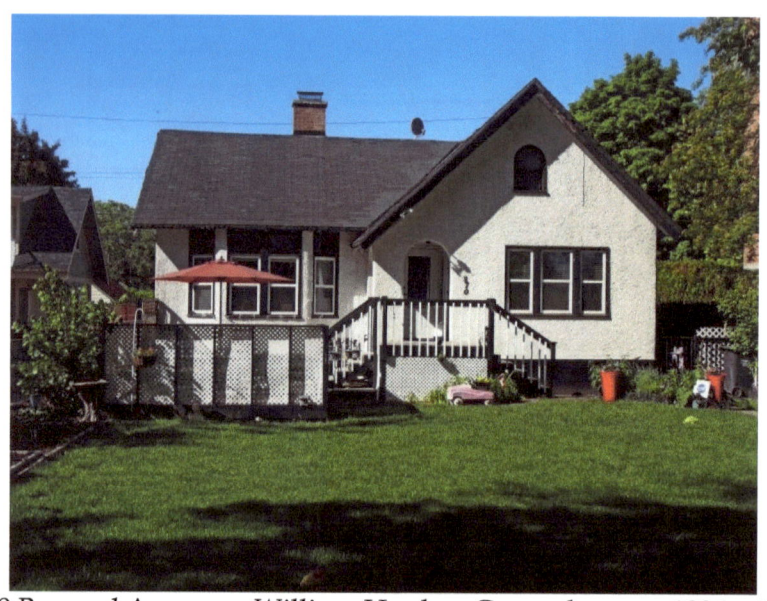

870 Bernard Avenue – William Hughes-Games house – 1936 – is a Vernacular Cottage with a cross-gabled roof. There is an arched opening to a recessed entry.

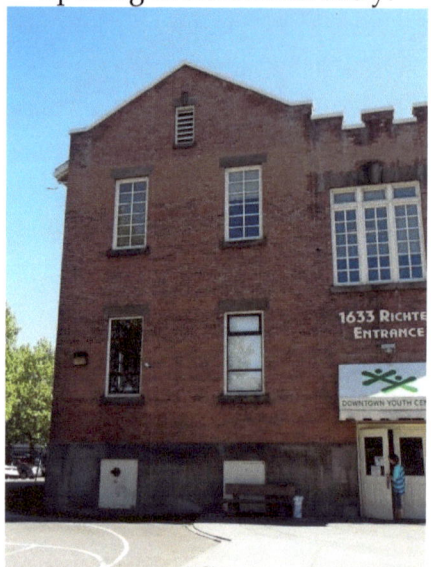

1633 Richter Street – Glenn Avenue School – 1910 – two-storey, six classrooms – Jacobethan Revival style – steeply pitched gable roof

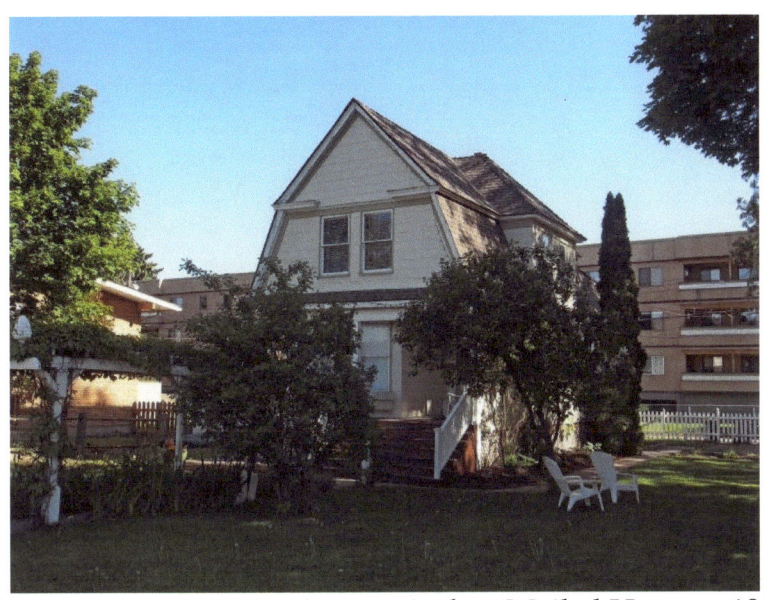

757 Lawrence Avenue – George Arthur Meikel House – 1910 – Dutch Colonial style – gambrel roof

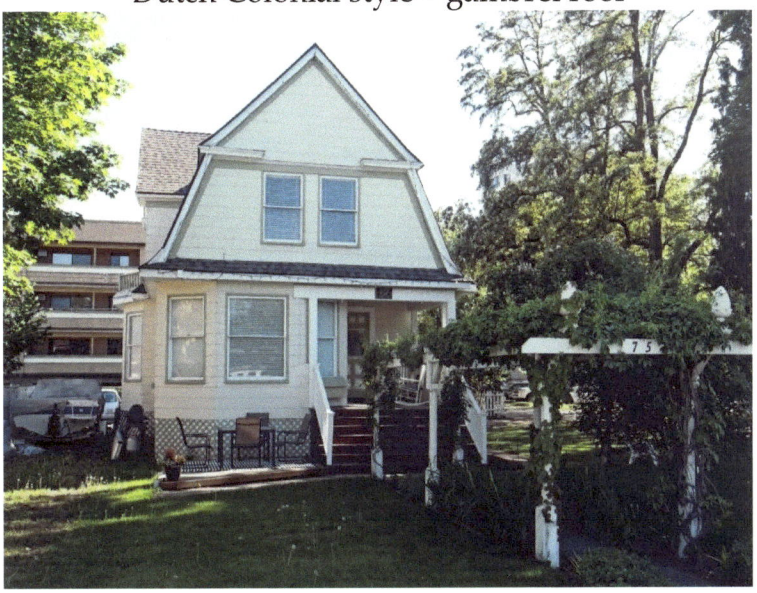

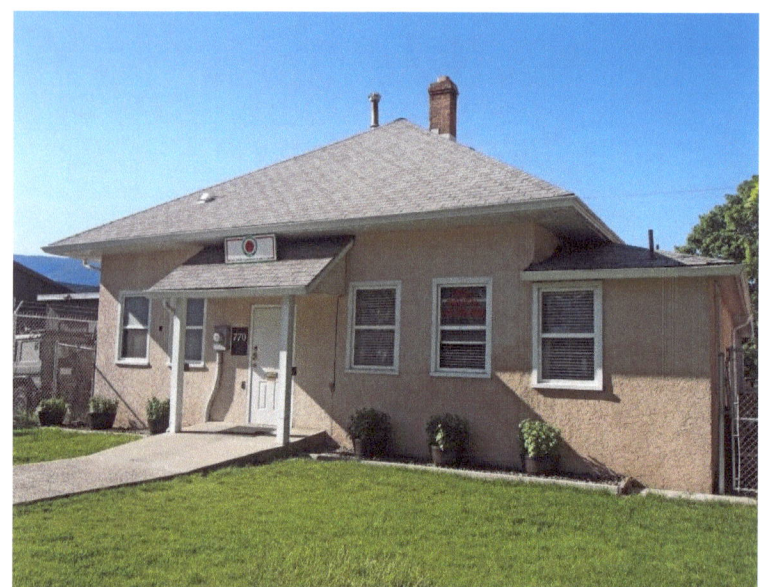

770 Lawrence Avenue – 1924 – W.C. Mitchell, the Manual Training teacher at Kelowna High School, constructed it with his students. In 1929 it became the Women's Institute Hall. Mary Pratten established a dance studio here in 1937.

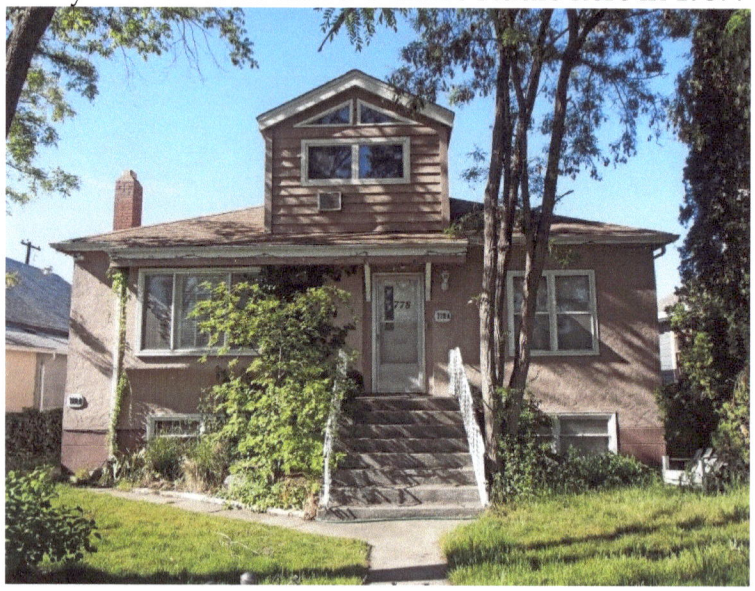

778 Lawrence Avenue

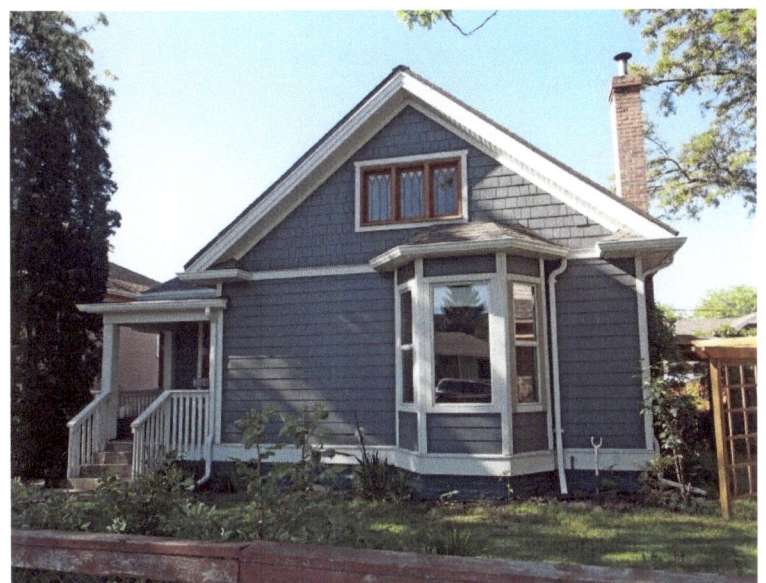

784 Lawrence Avenue – Trench House – 1911 – Arts and Crafts style – William Trench was a pharmacist.

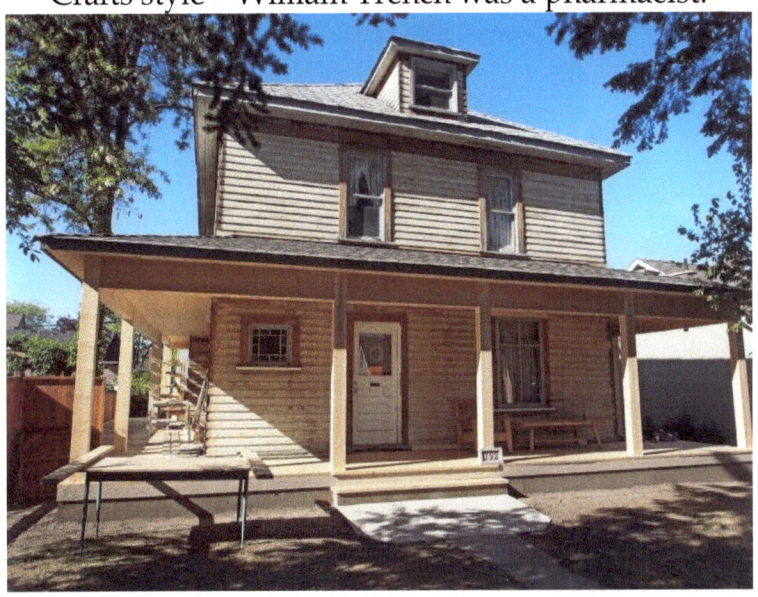

792 Lawrence Avenue – Collins House – 1910 - Victorian Revival, foursquare design

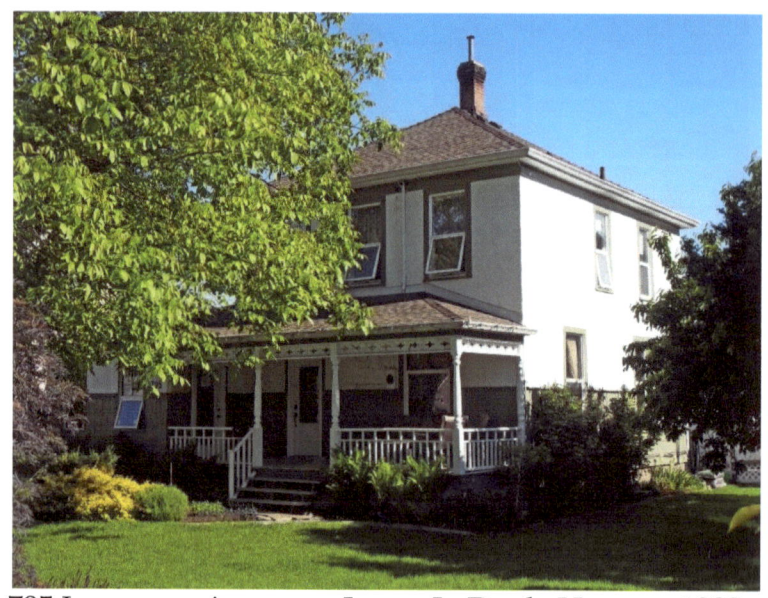

795 Lawrence Avenue – James L. Doyle House – 1908 – foursquare style, two-storey height

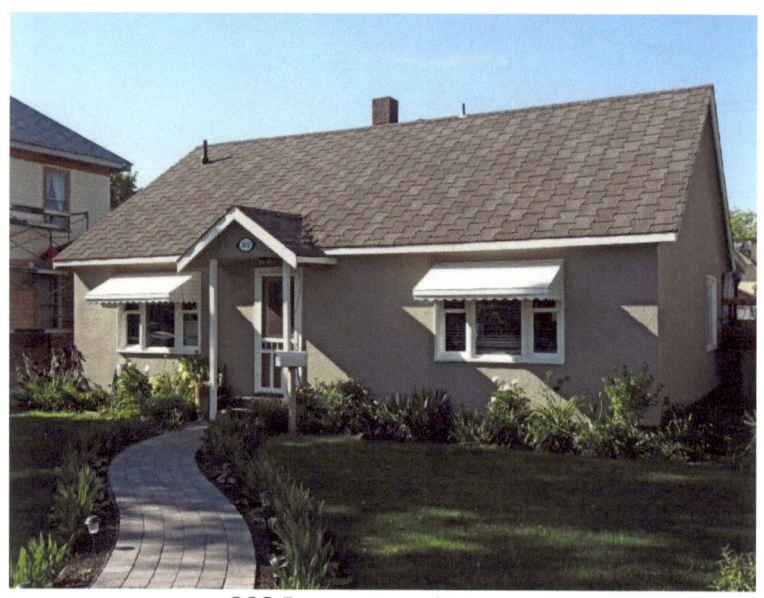

802 Lawrence Avenue

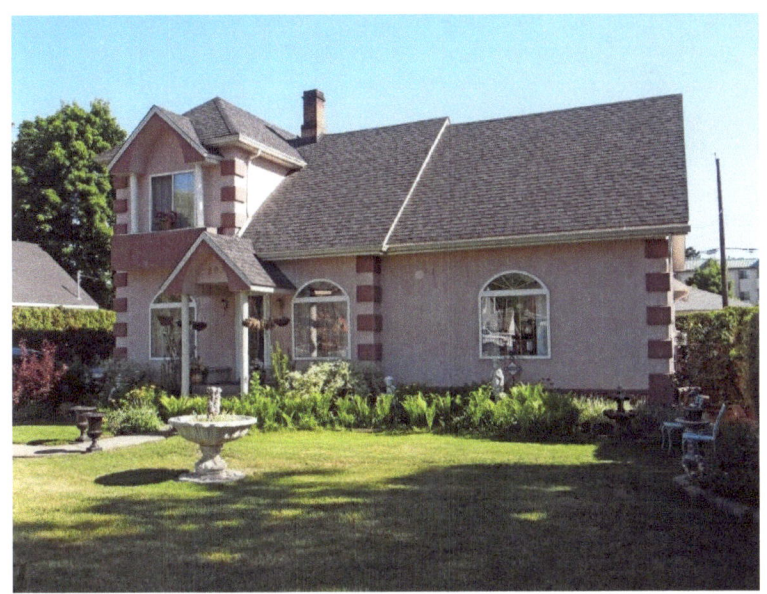

803 Lawrence Avenue

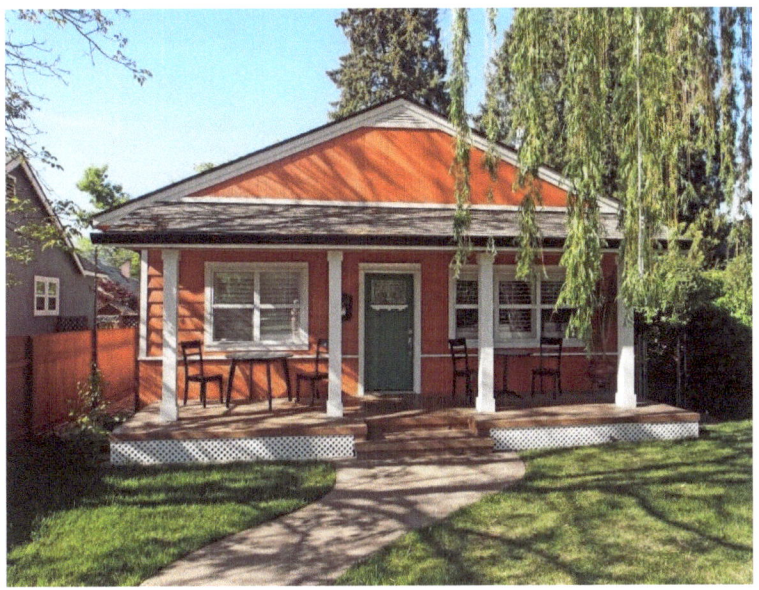

814 Lawrence Avenue

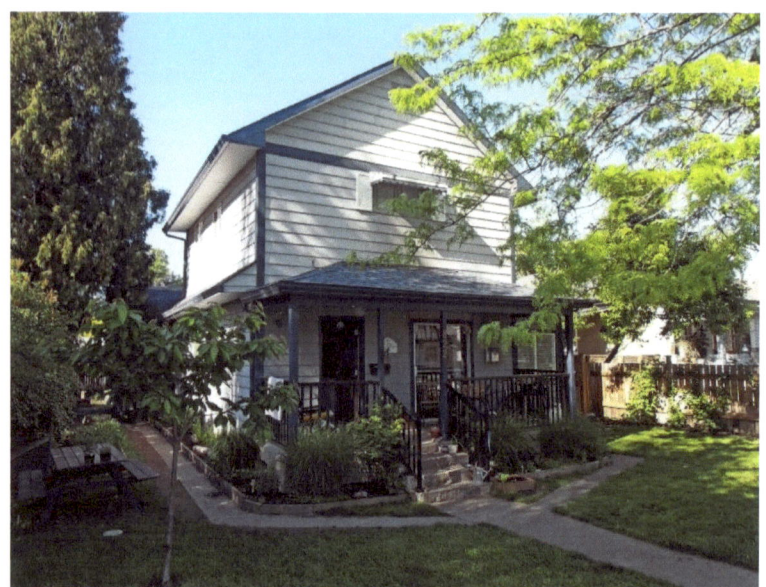

822 Lawrence Avenue – Sarah H. Frank House – 1901 – Homestead Vernacular – gable roof, heavy eaves

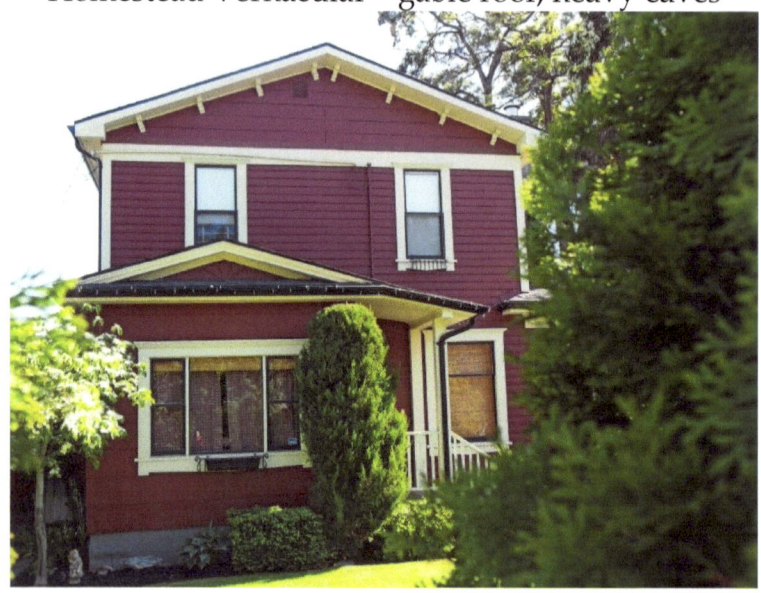

825 Lawrence Avenue – Brunette House – 1906 – Vernacular – two-storey height, gable over second floor with deep eaves supported by wooden brackets, horizontal wood siding

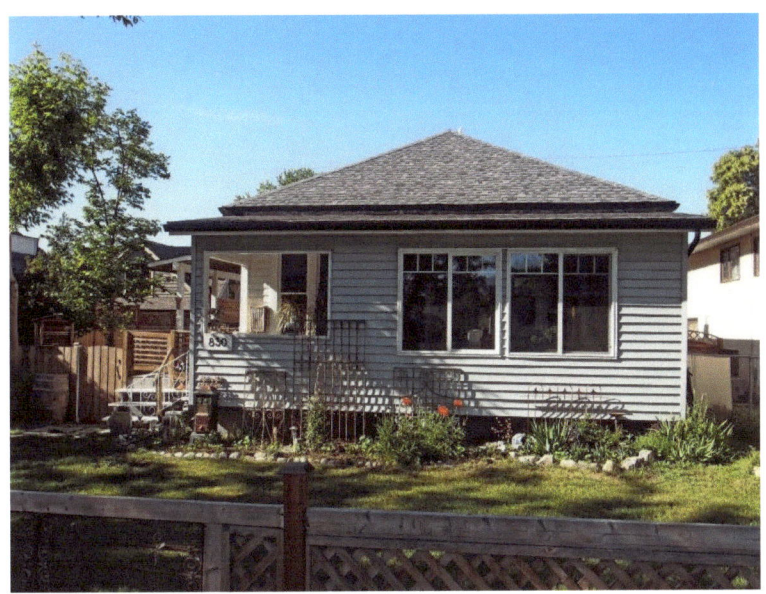

830 Lawrence Avenue

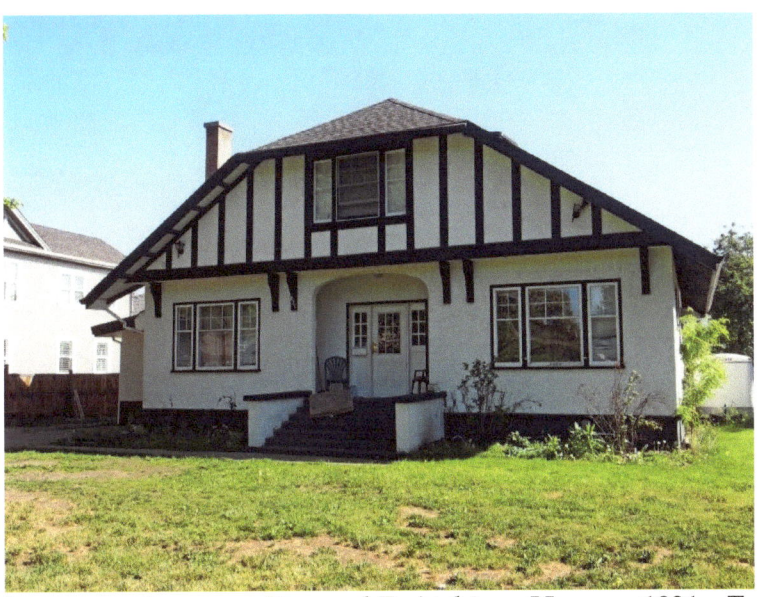

831 Lawrence Avenue – Howard E. Atchison House – 1931 – Tudor Revival style with half-timber detailing on stucco, gable roof truncated at the peak

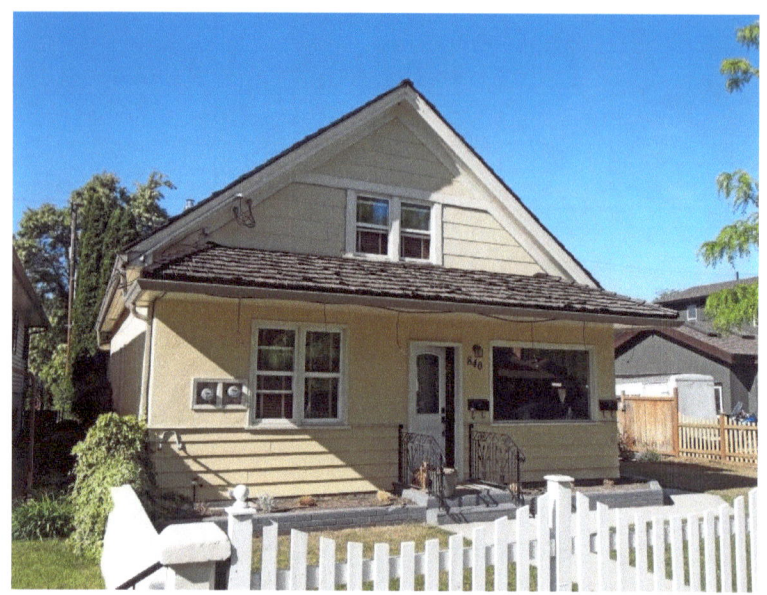

840 Lawrence Avenue

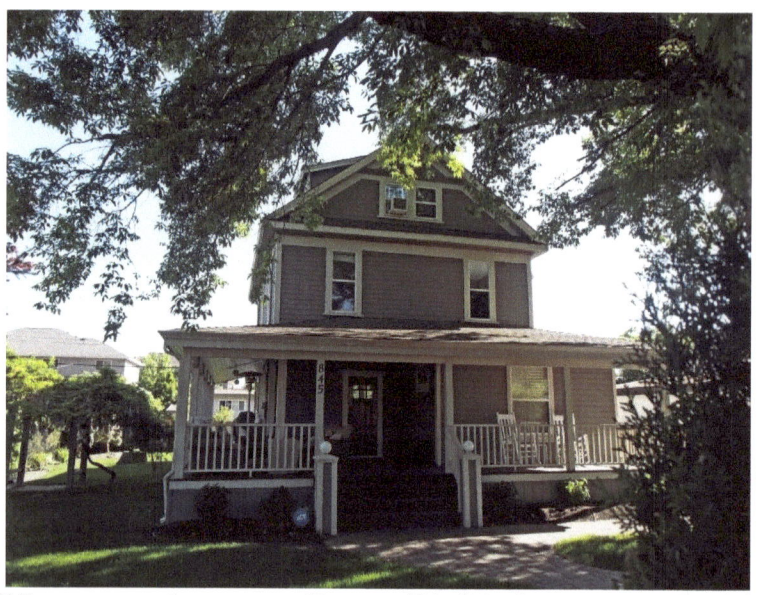

845 Lawrence Avenue – George Ritchie (contractor, builder) House – 1907 – wood frame home with gable roof, wraparound veranda

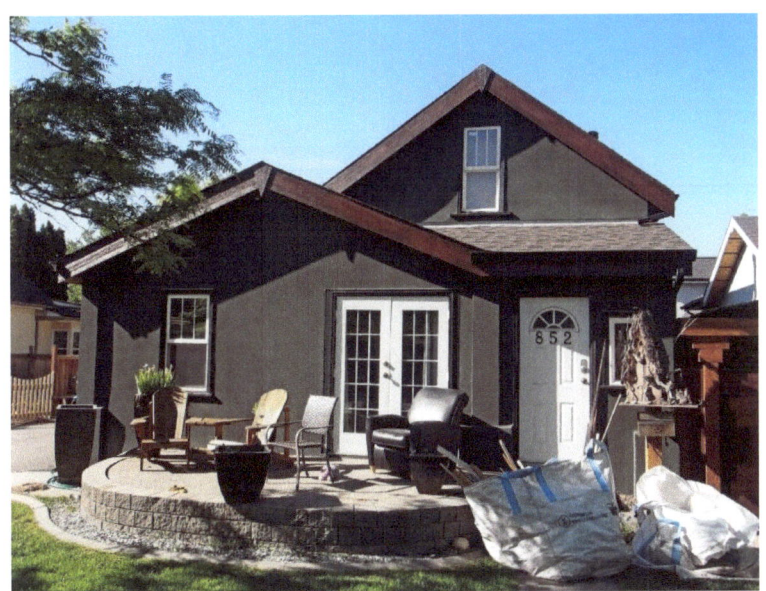

852 Lawrence Avenue

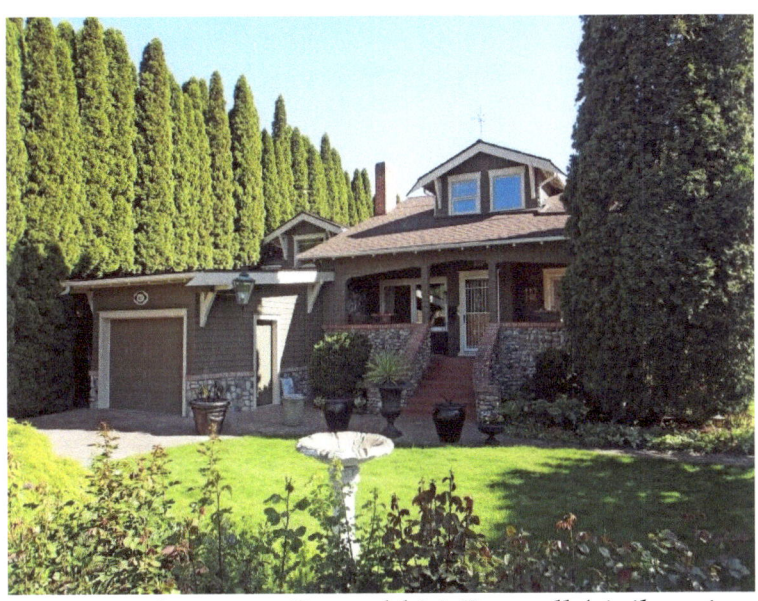

857 Lawrence Avenue – Dougald McDougall (civil engineer in fruit industry) House – 1922 – California Craftsman Bungalow – gable roof with deep eaves and exposed rafters, deep porch

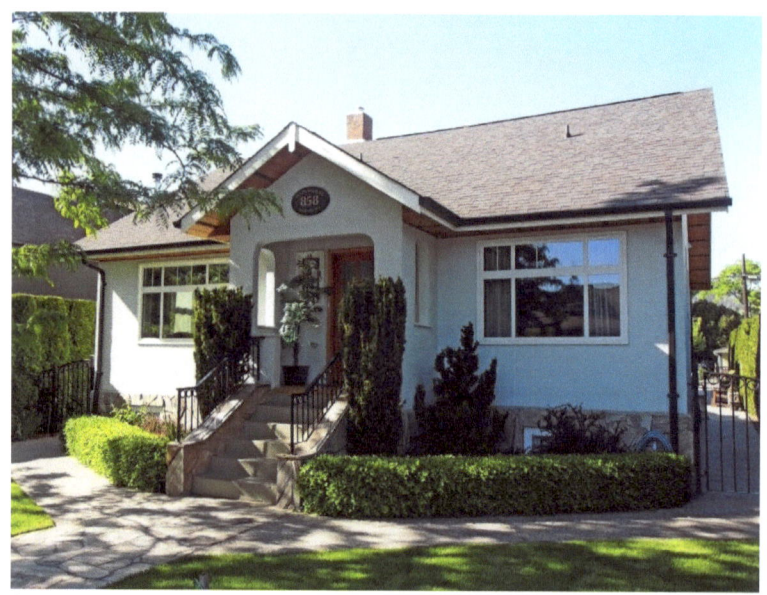

858 Lawrence Avenue – John Peter "Jack" Minette House – 1947 – Post Second World War style – 1½-storeys, full basement, side-gabled roof, front projecting entryway with arched openings

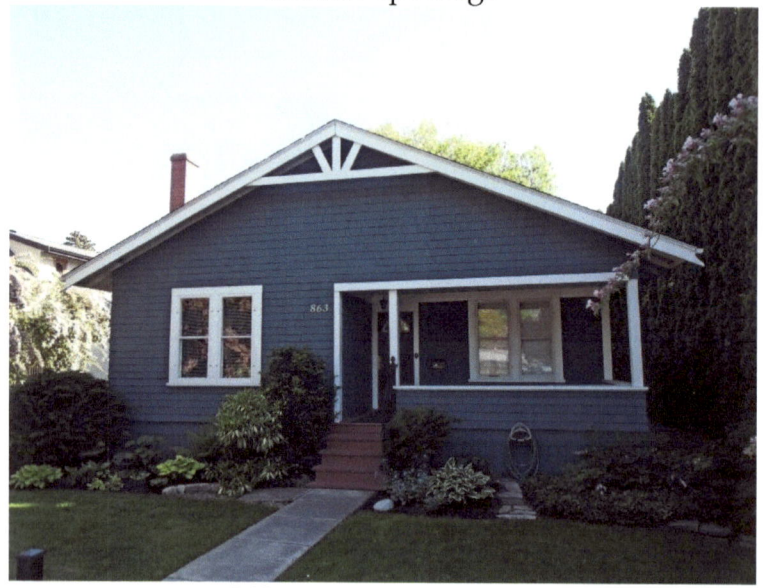

863 Lawrence Avenue

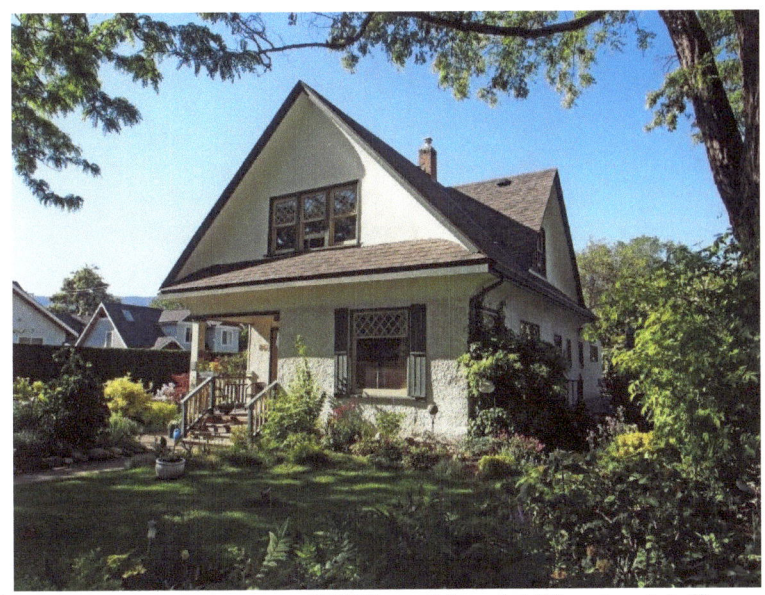

868 Lawrence Avenue – William Harold Hunter McDougall (fruit grower and exporter) House – 1909 – Vernacular Cottage style

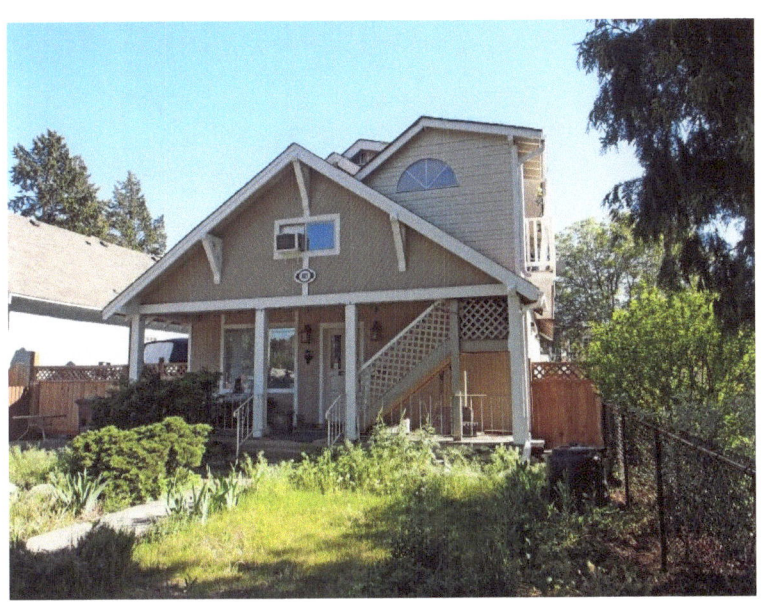

883 Lawrence Avenue

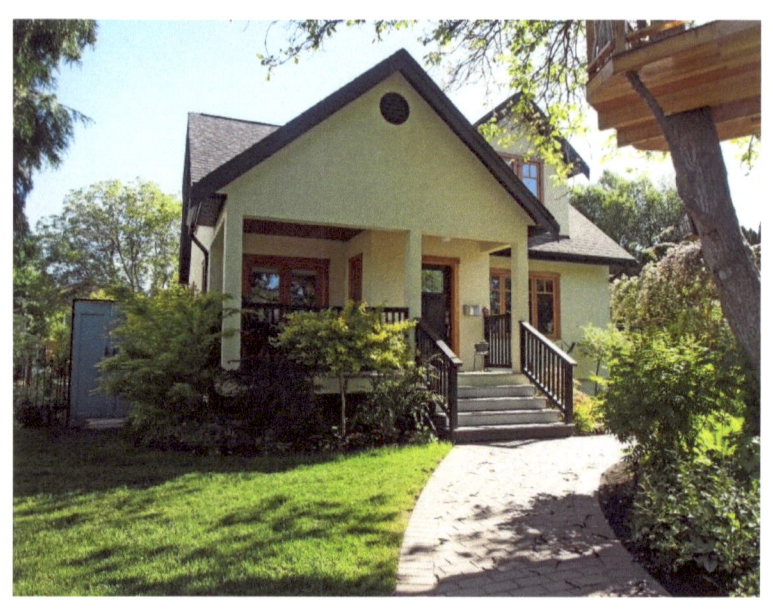

875 Lawrence Avenue - treehouse

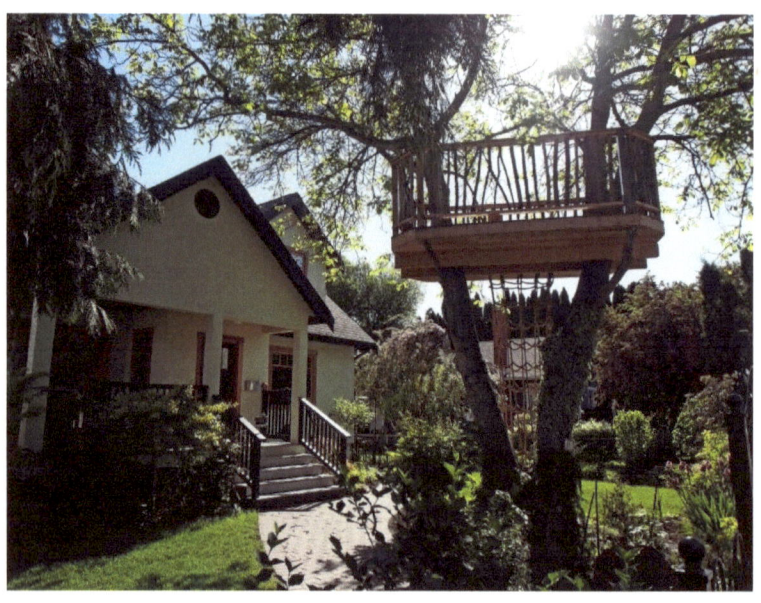

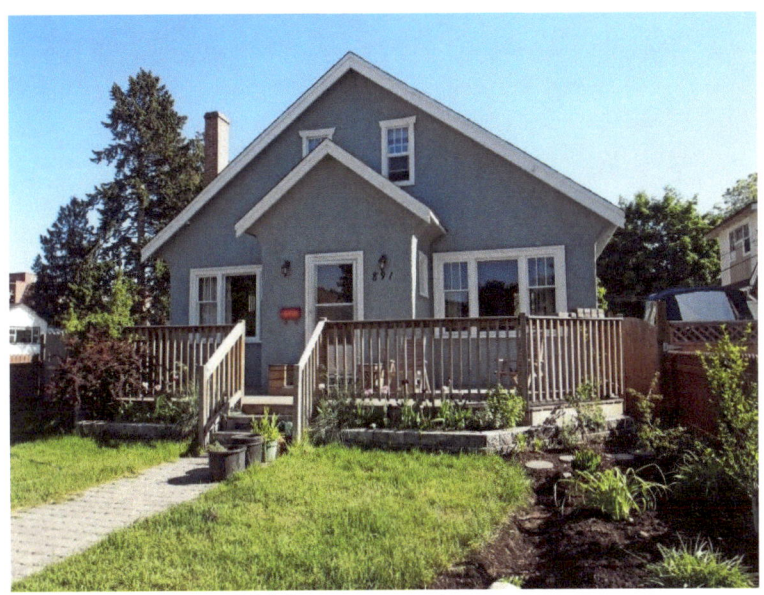

891 Lawrence Avenue

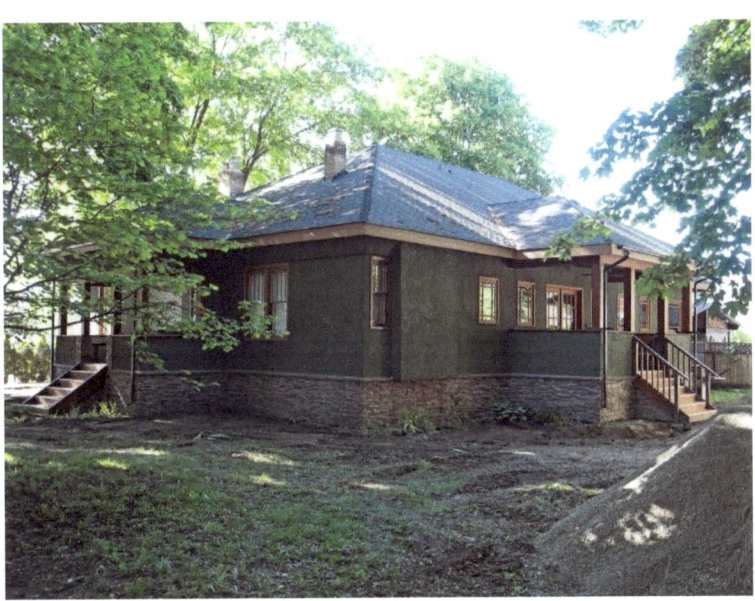

Lawrence Avenue

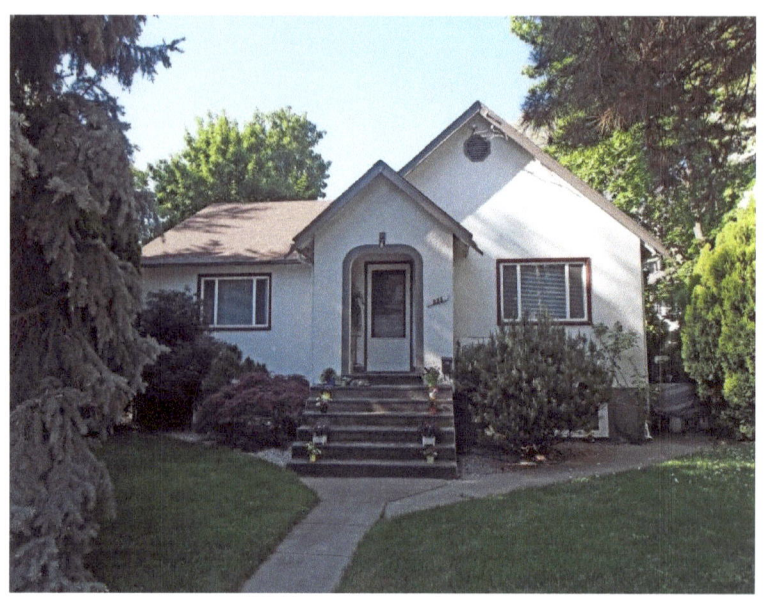

958 Lawrence Avenue

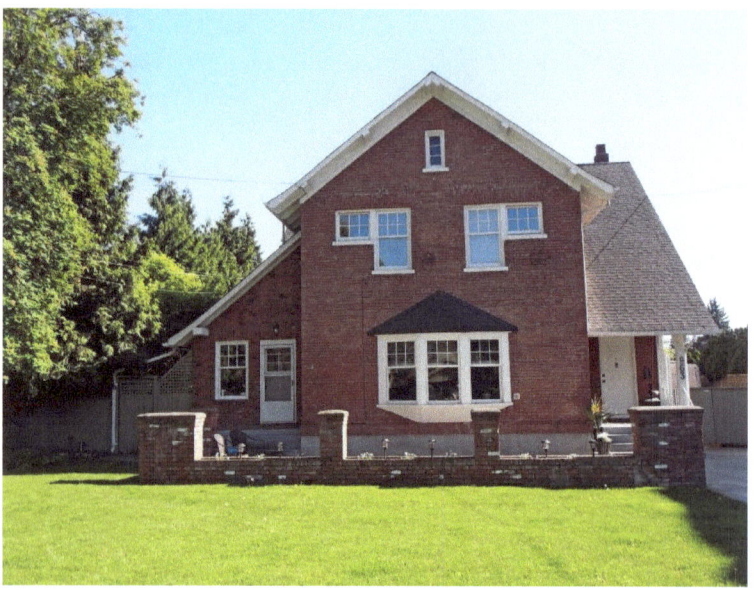

963 Lawrence Avenue – United Church Manse – 1913 – Craftsman influence shown in bay window

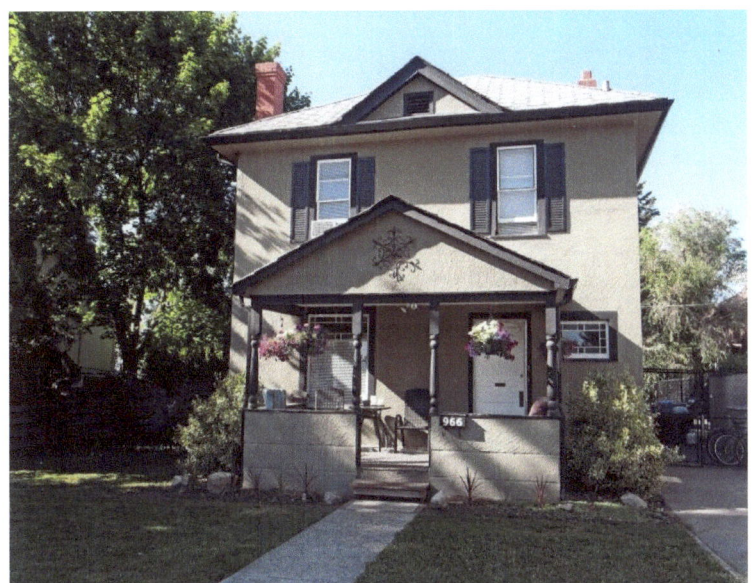

966 Lawrence Avenue – Munson House – 1911 – Victorian Foursquare with hipped roof, gabled dormer and covered porch – Robert Munson was a sawmill worker.

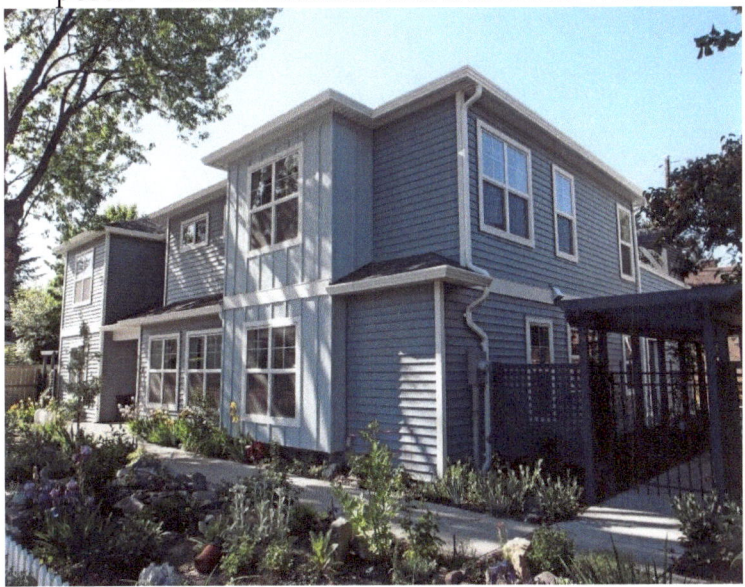

Lawrence Avenue

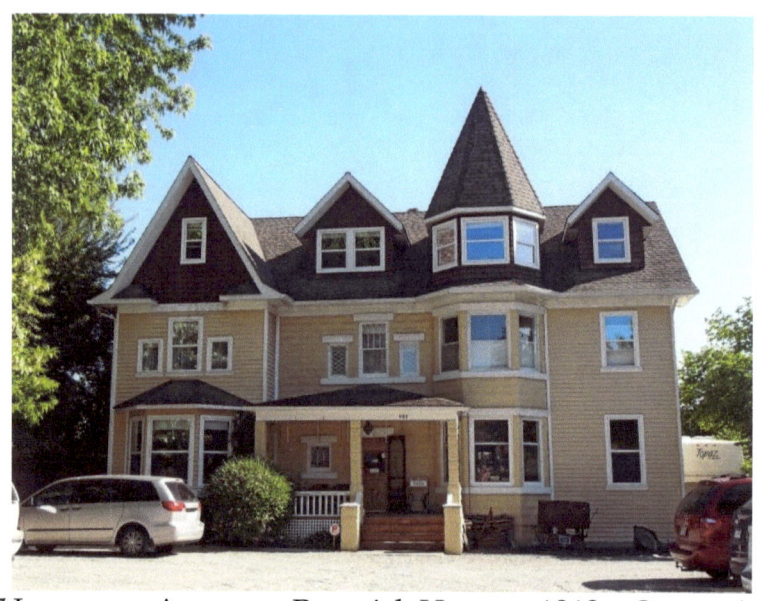

987 Lawrence Avenue – Renwick House – 1912 – Queen Anne style – altered from the original – turret, bay window, dormers

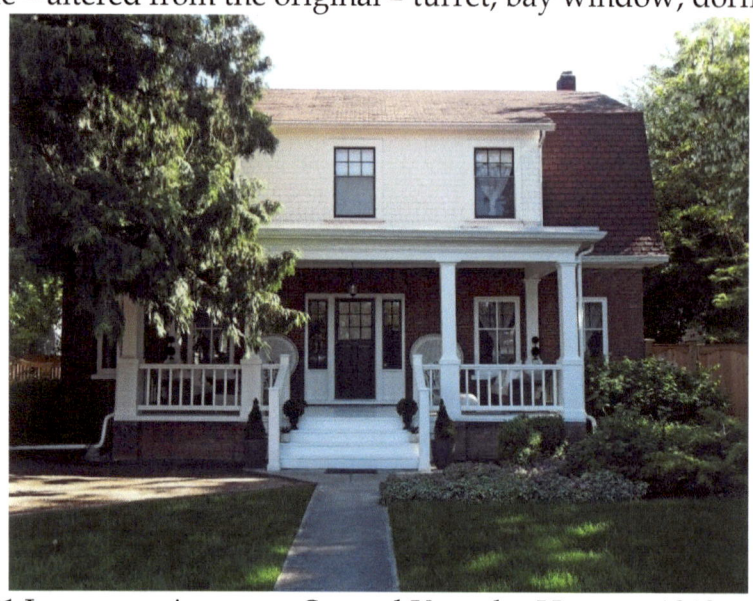

1001 Lawrence Avenue – Second Knowles House – 1913 – J. B. Knowles was a jeweller and civic leader. Dutch Colonial Revival style – gambrel roof

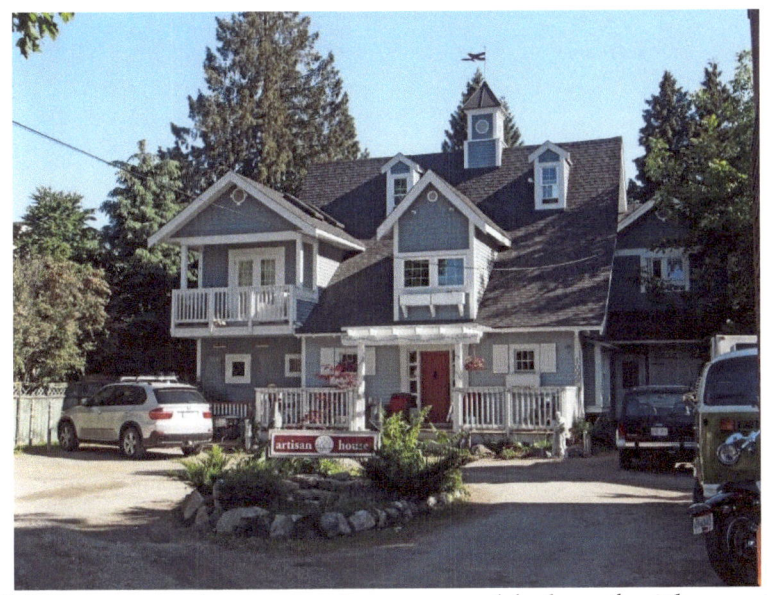

1009 Lawrence Avenue – dormers, gabled roof with cupola, second floor balcony

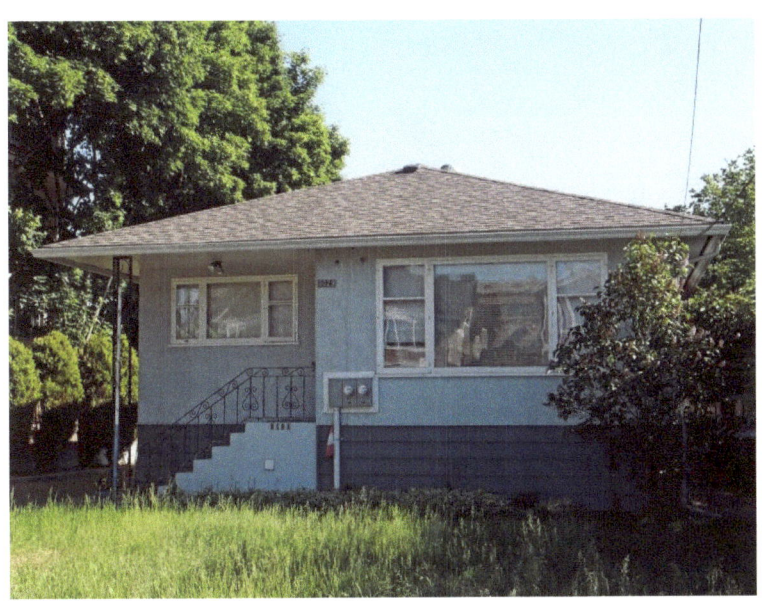

1029 Lawrence Avenue

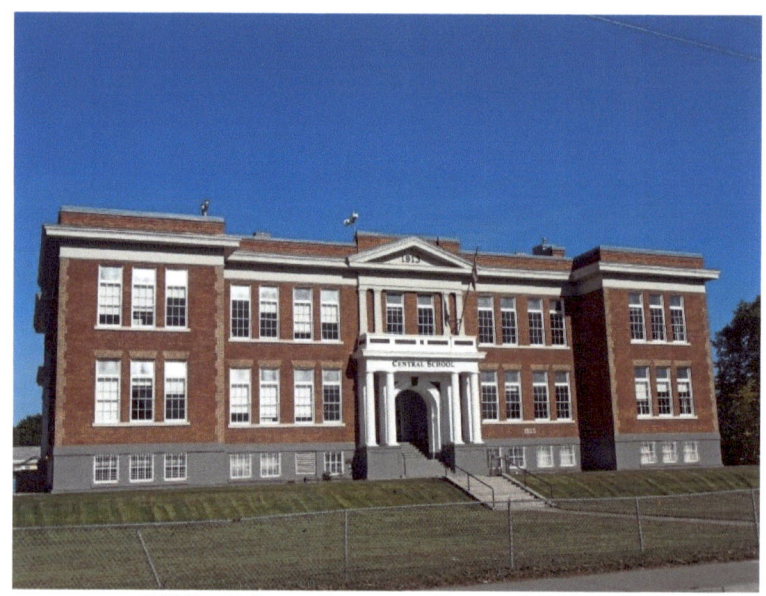

1825 Richter Street – Central School

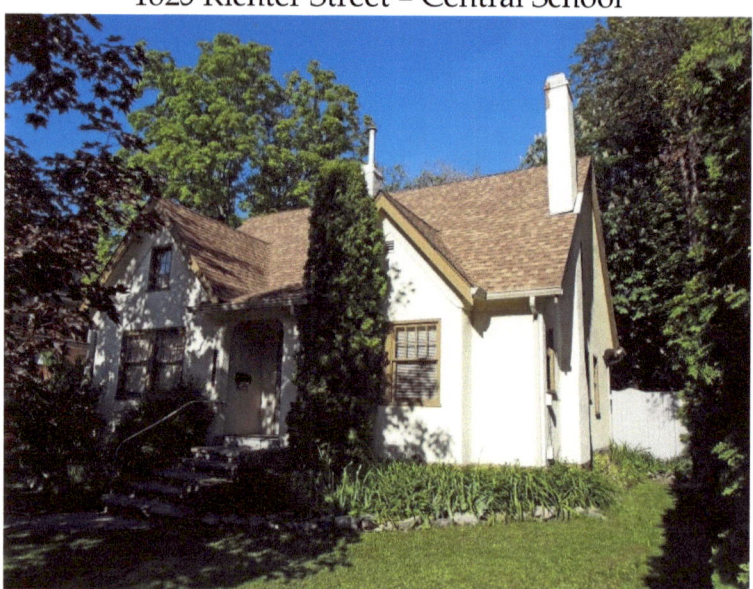

1807 Marshall Street – Percy Harding (ran a hardware store) House – Mid-Wars Cottage style – 1929 – 1½ storeys with basement, rectangular plan - wood-frame construction with smooth stucco exterior cladding, multi-paned windows

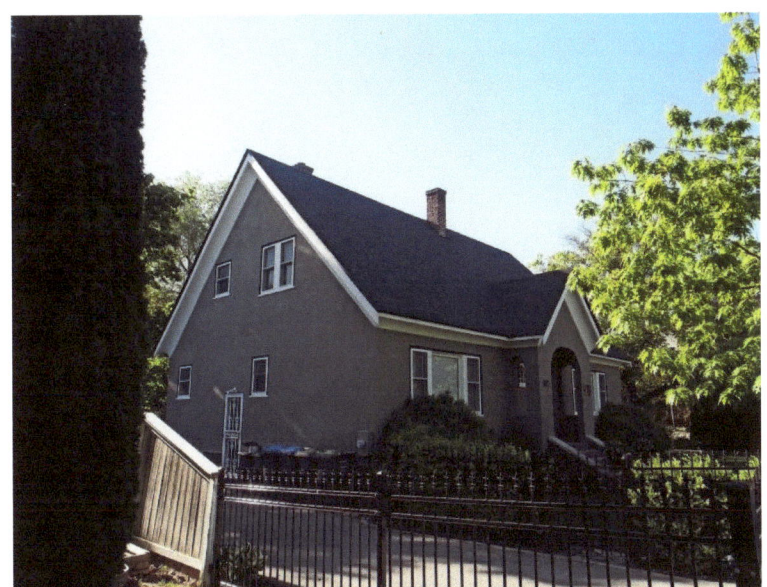

1812 Marshall Street – Staples House – early Vernacular Cottage – 1931 – between-the-wars cottage style – clean lines, simple symmetrical street elevation, steep gable roof

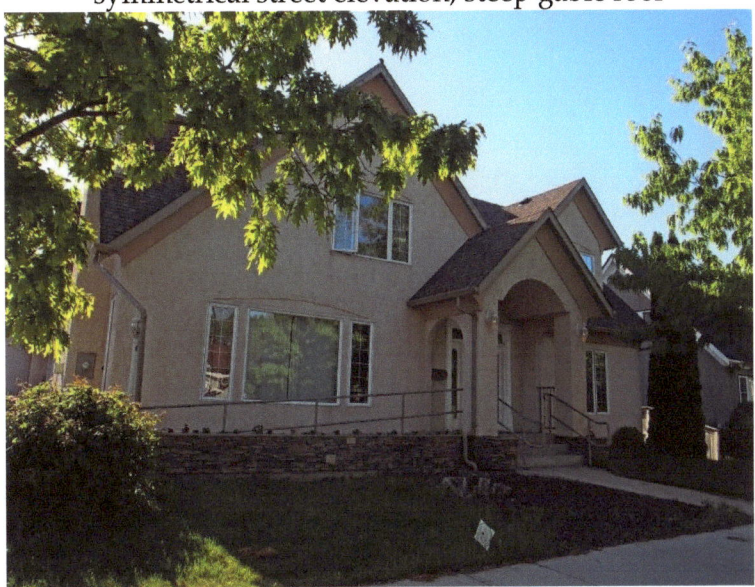

1820 Marshall Street – built by Mr. and Mrs. Kievil – they loved flowers and gardening and bought a lot and a half to fill with trees, shrubs, roses, and all kinds of flowers.

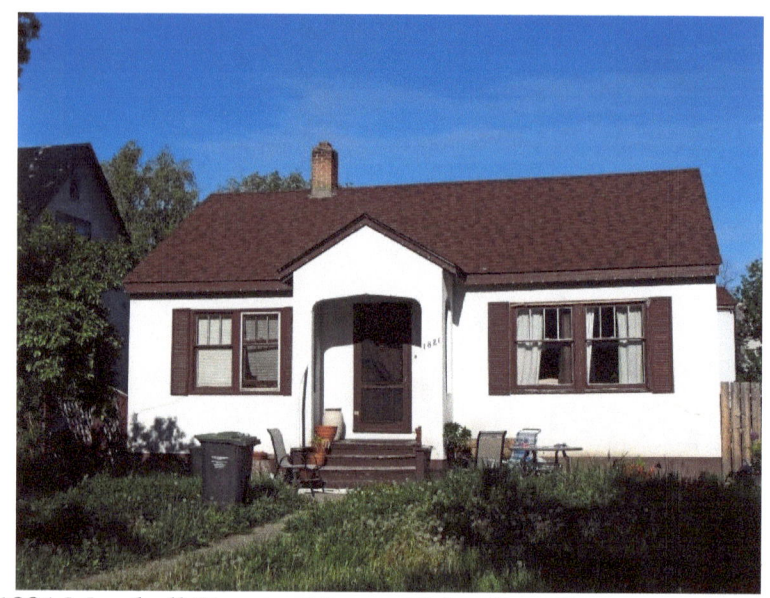

1821 Marshall Street – Mr. and Mrs. Ron Prosser – owned Victory Motors car dealership

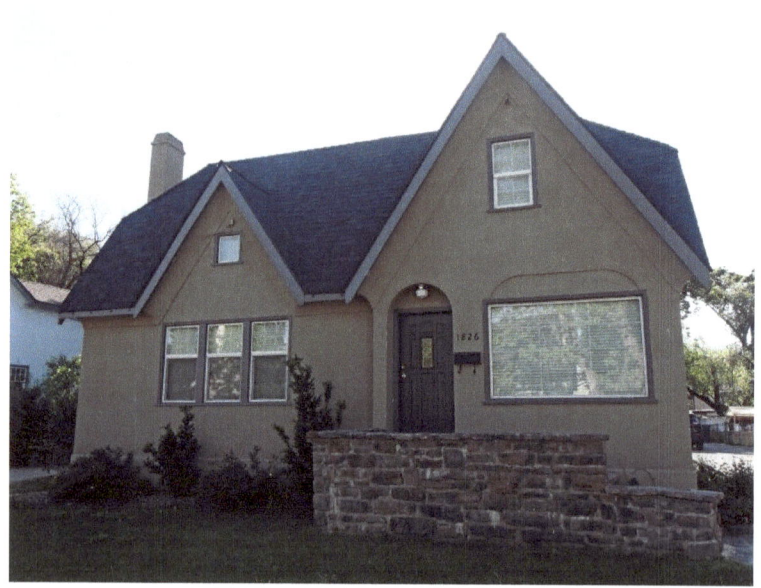

1826 Marshall Street – Mr. J.L. Burnham (agent for the C.P.R.) House – 1930 – early Vernacular Cottage

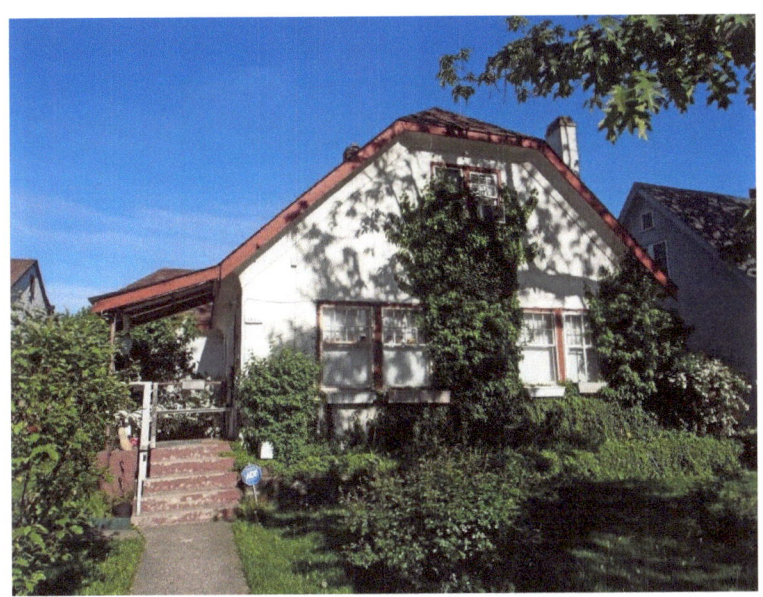

1827 Marshall Street – Stewart House

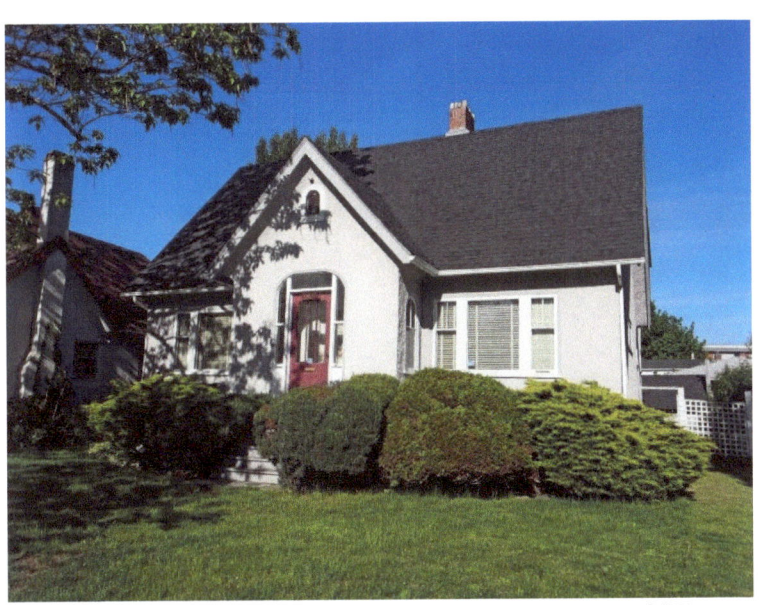

1835 Marshall Street – Delcourt House - 1937

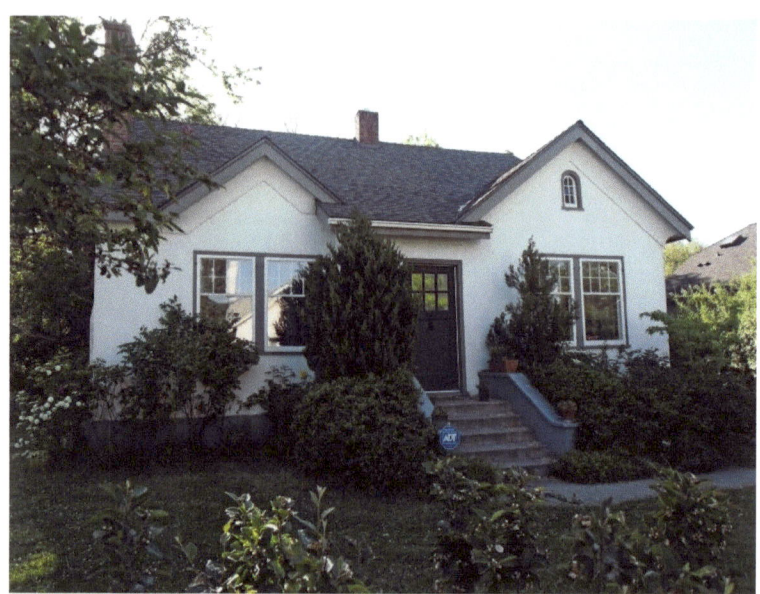

1842 Marshall Street – Mr. Maurice Matson (mining engineer at the Beaverdell Silver Mine) House

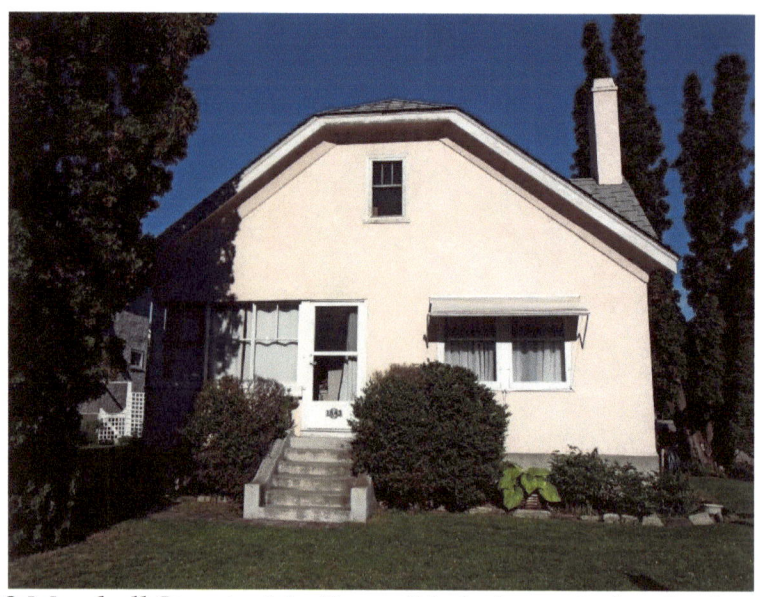

1843 Marshall Street – Mr. Bruce Little (captain for the ferries) House

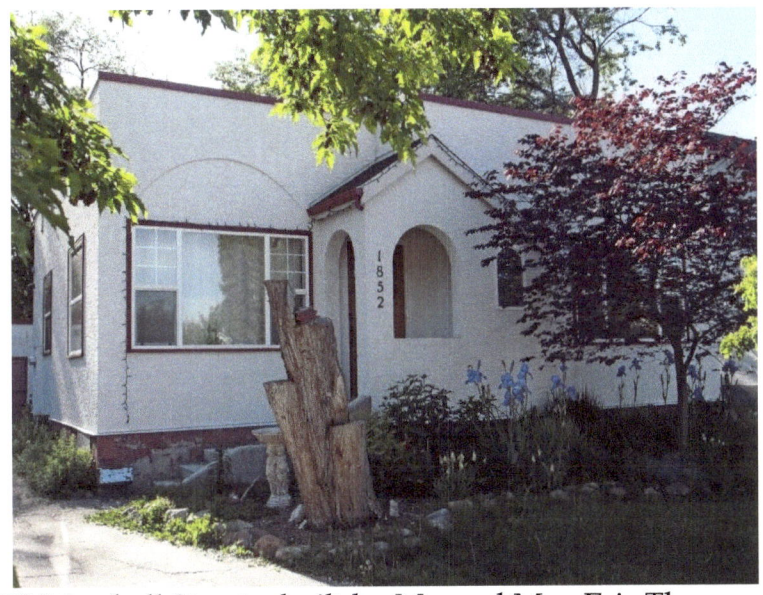

1852 Marshall Street – built by Mr. and Mrs. Eric Thompson, jewellers

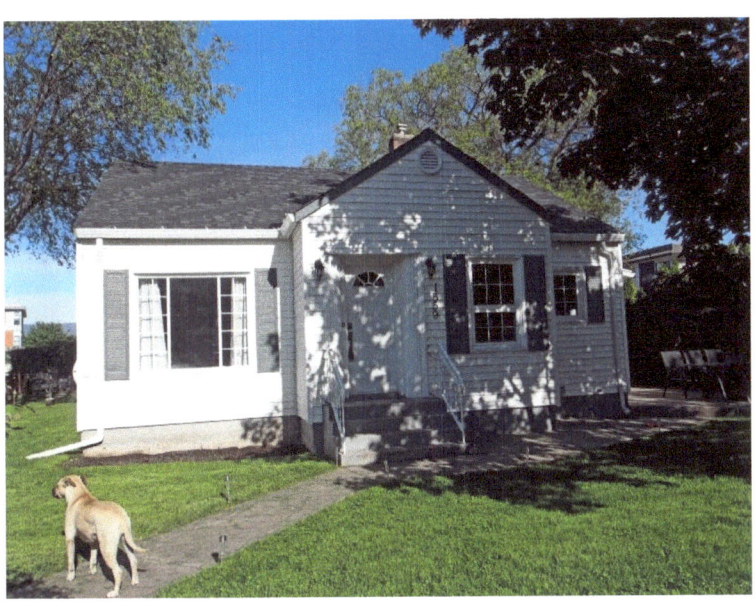

1859 Marshall Street

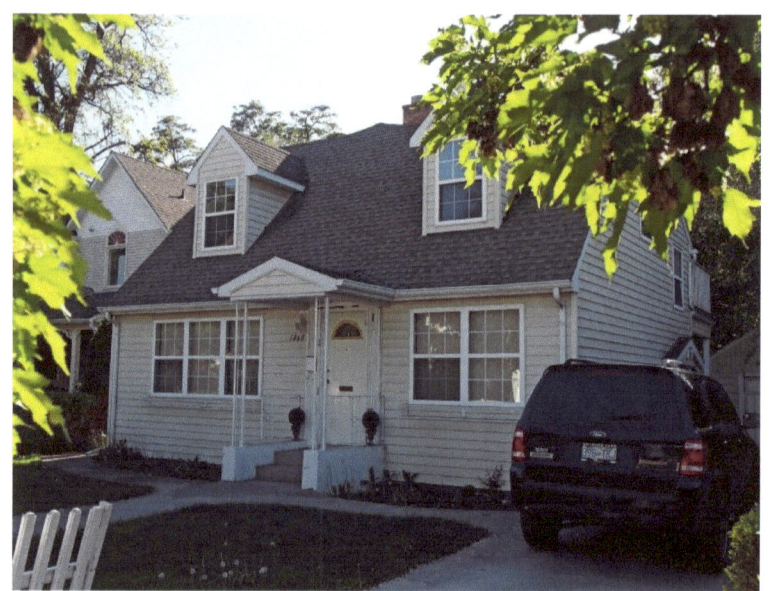

1860 Marshall Street

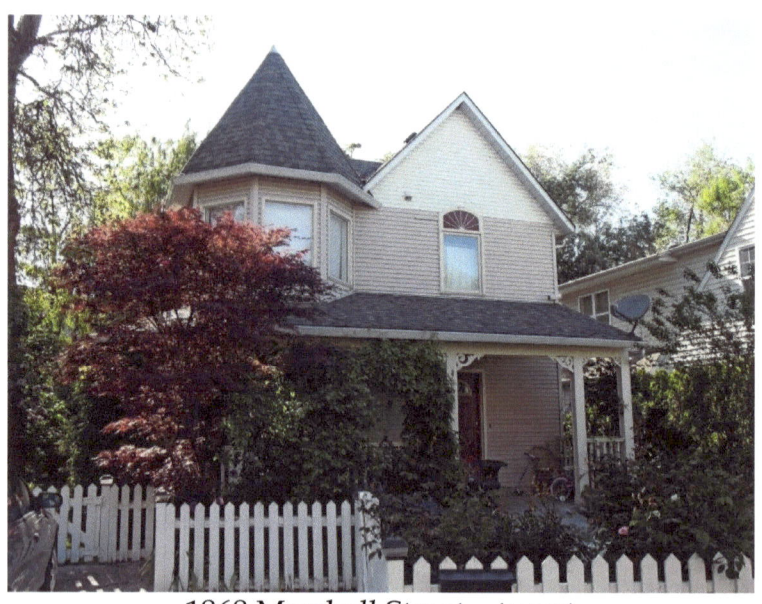

1868 Marshall Street – turret

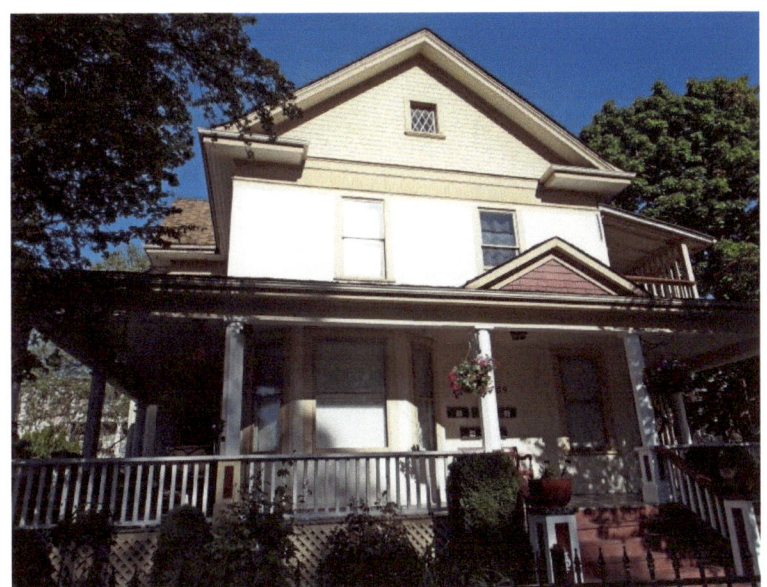

1869 Marshall Street – William John Marshall (dairy farmer) House – 1908 – late Queen Anne elements, foursquare character – wraparound veranda, classical columns, balustrades and stick work details, pediment over entry

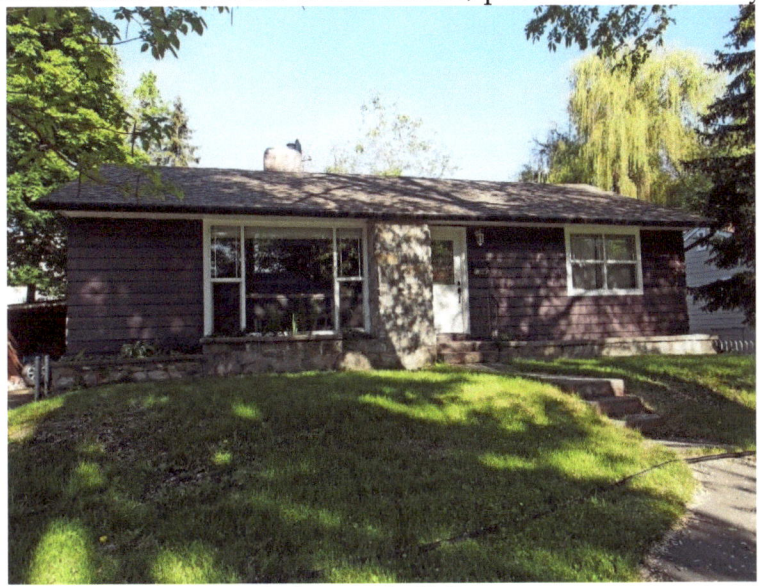

1879 Marshall Street

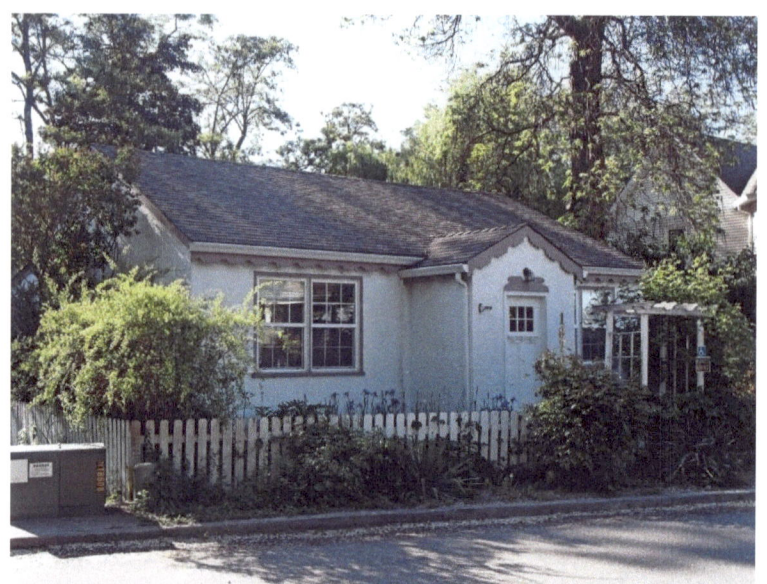

1876 Marshall Street – The Gibb House (they ran the Gibb Grocery in the North End) – Mid-War Vernacular Cottage – 1930s - projecting entry at the center of the house with a small gable roof (now enclosed)

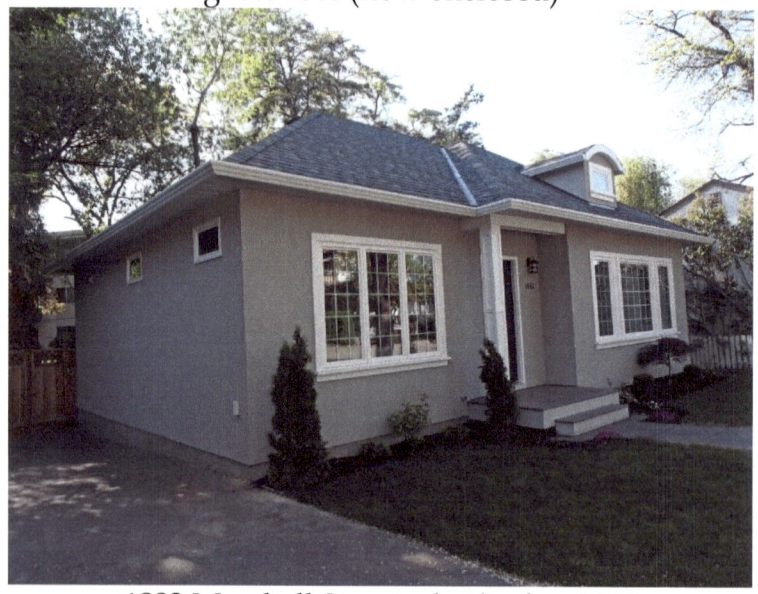

1882 Marshall Street – built after 1950

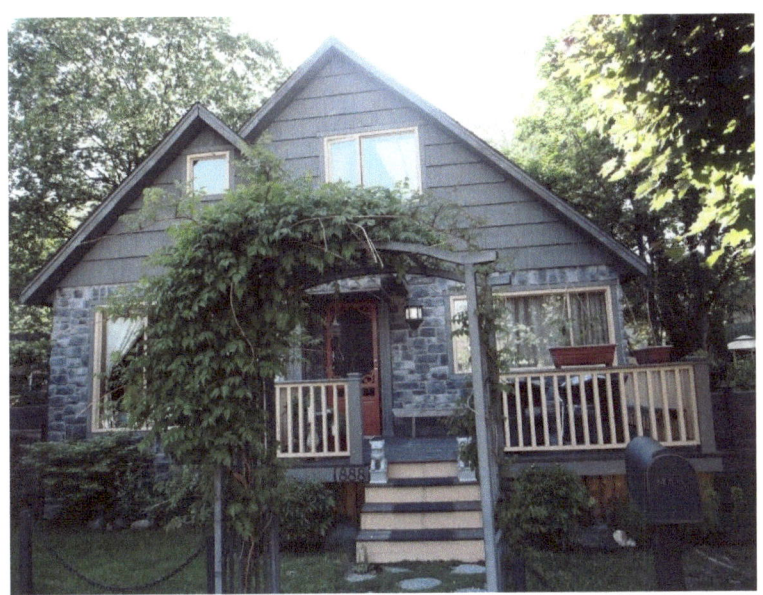

1888 Marshall Street

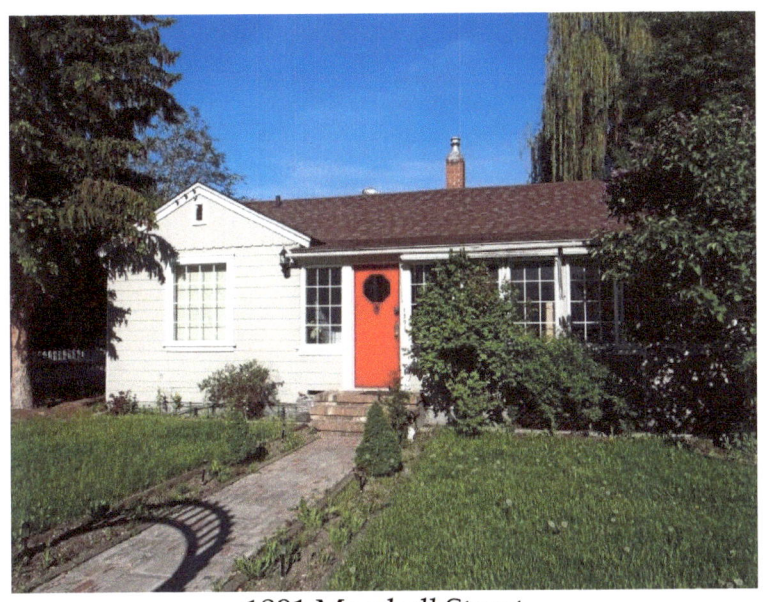

1891 Marshall Street

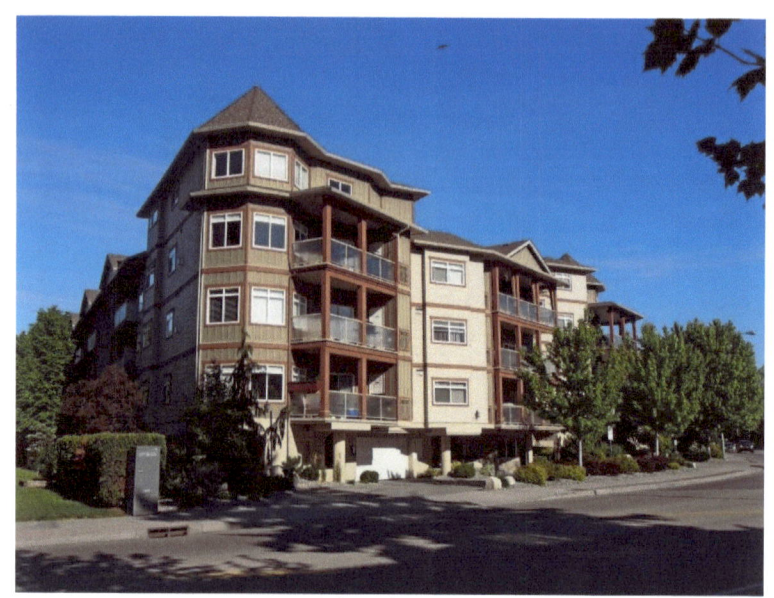

Buckland Avenue

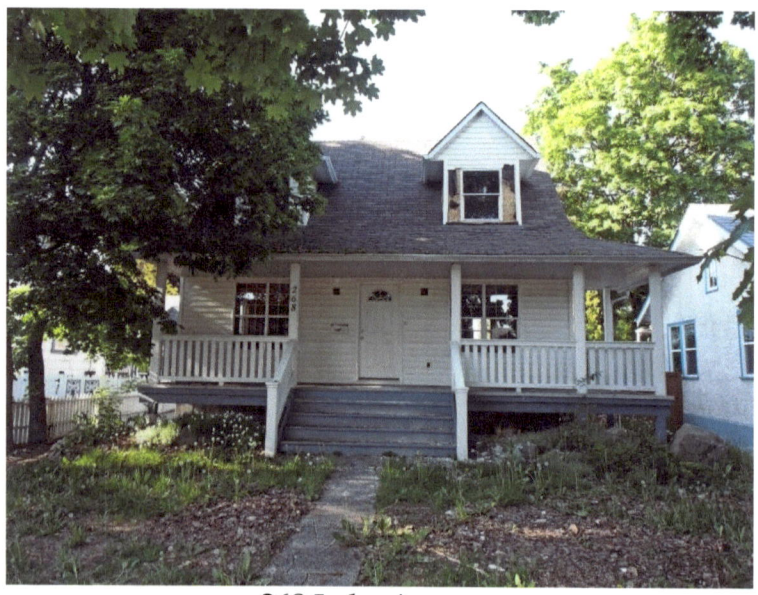

268 Lake Avenue

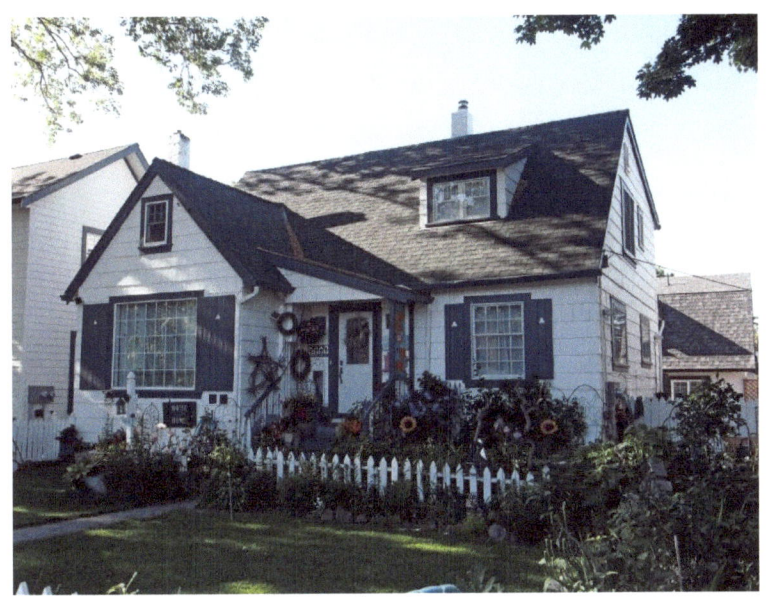

262 Lake Avenue

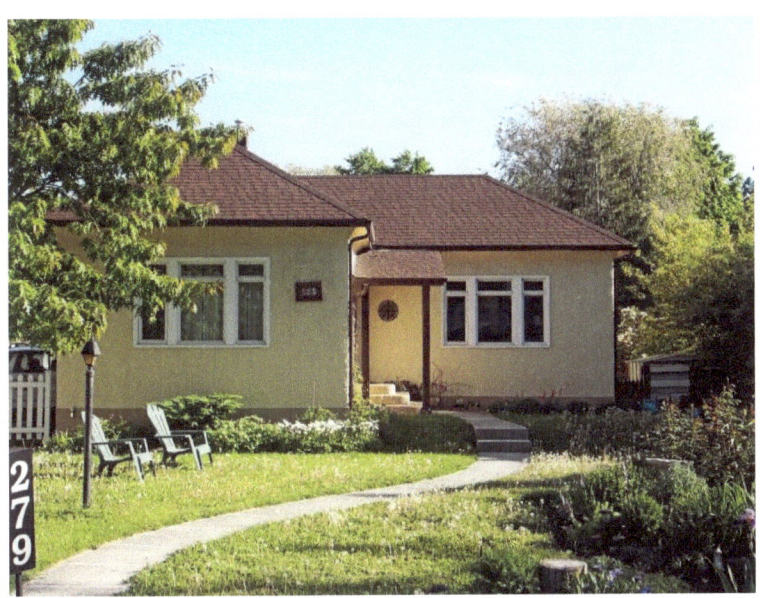

279 Lake Avenue

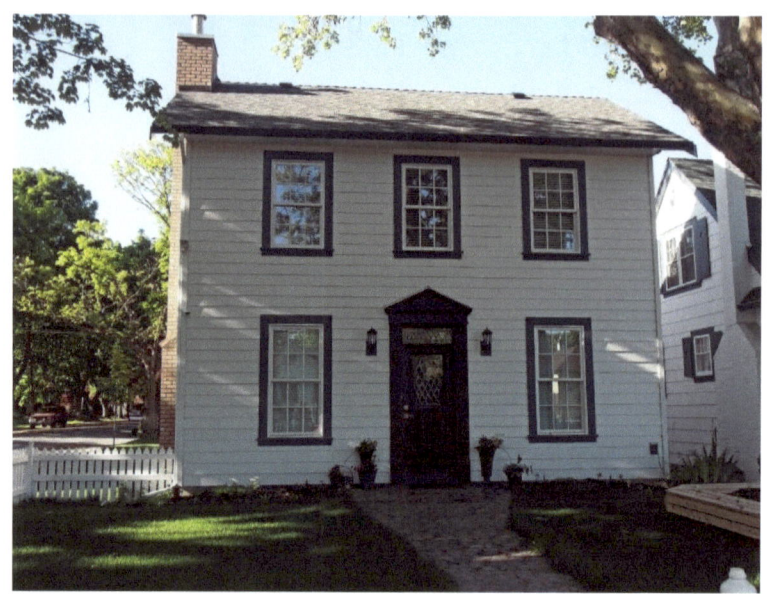

250 Lake Avenue

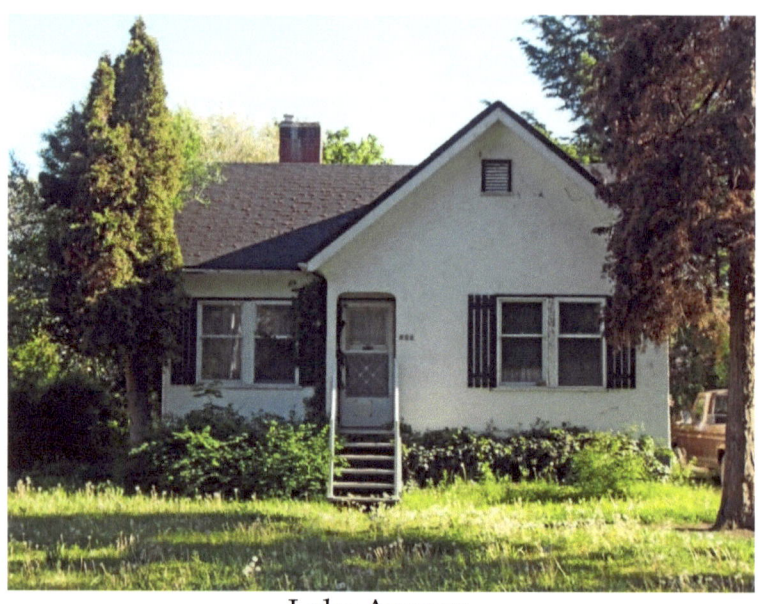

Lake Avenue

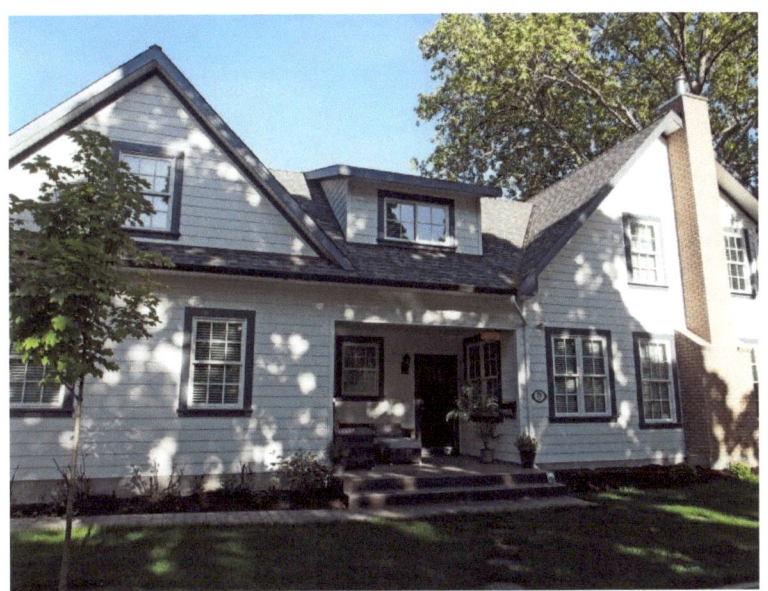

250 Lake Avenue

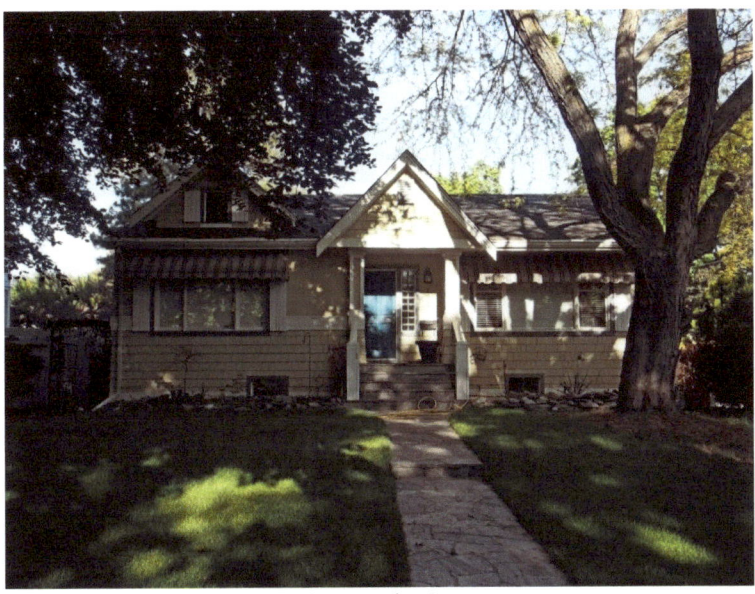

1879 Maple Street

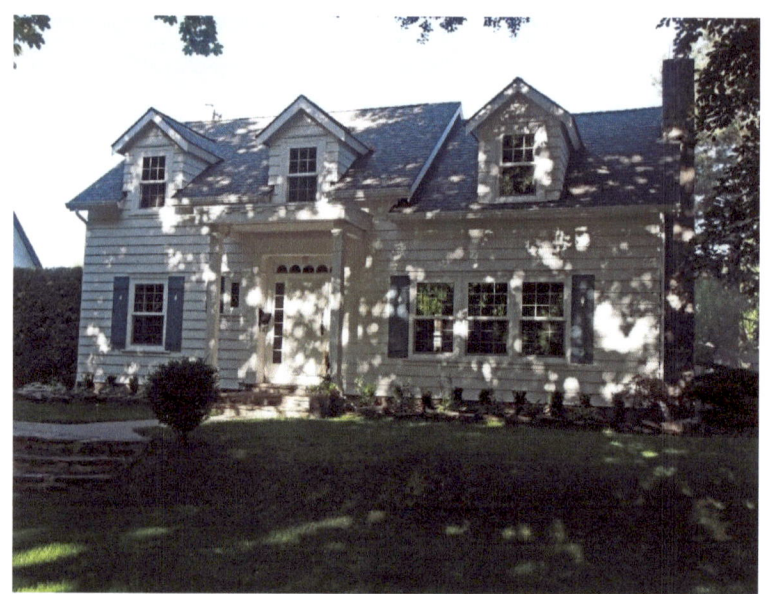

1869 Maple Street – A. Patterson Roy MacLean (publishers and managing editor of the Kelowna Courier) House – 1942 – Georgian Revival style – gable roof, horizontal siding, grand entrance, vertical multi-sash windows with shutters, symmetrical front

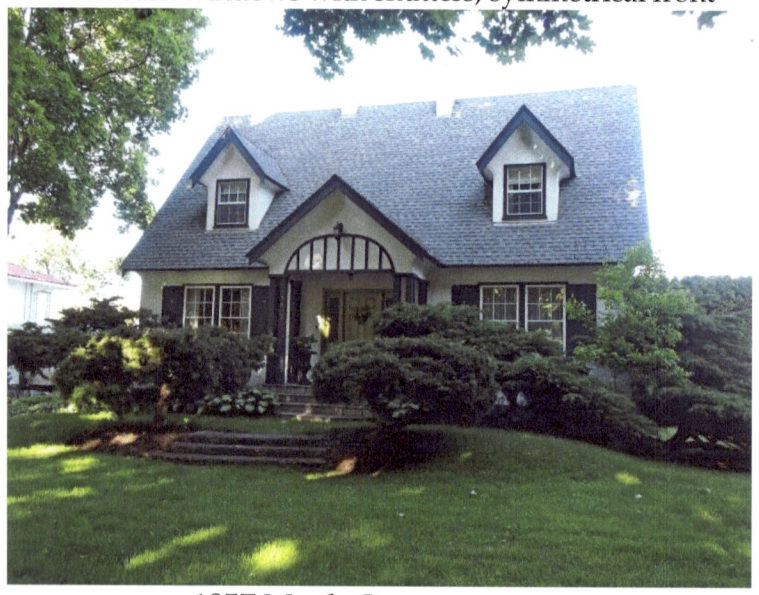

1857 Maple Street - cottage

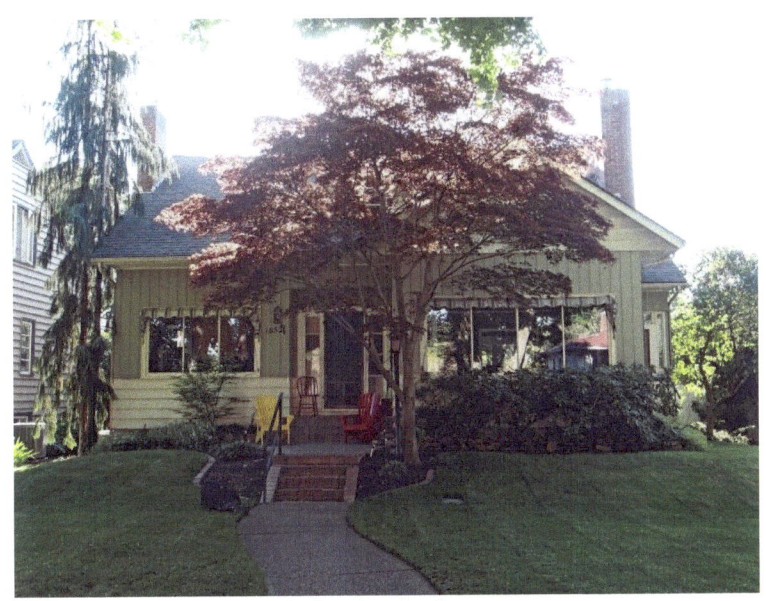

1852 Maple Street

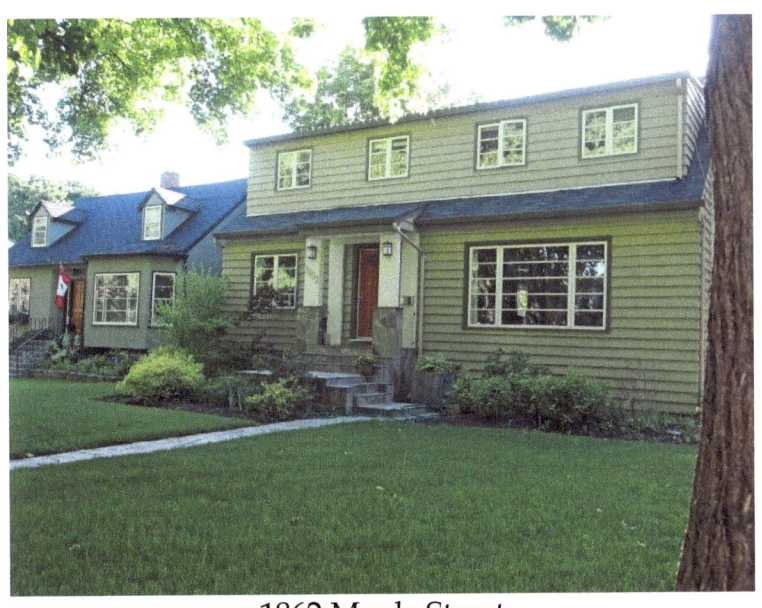

1862 Maple Street

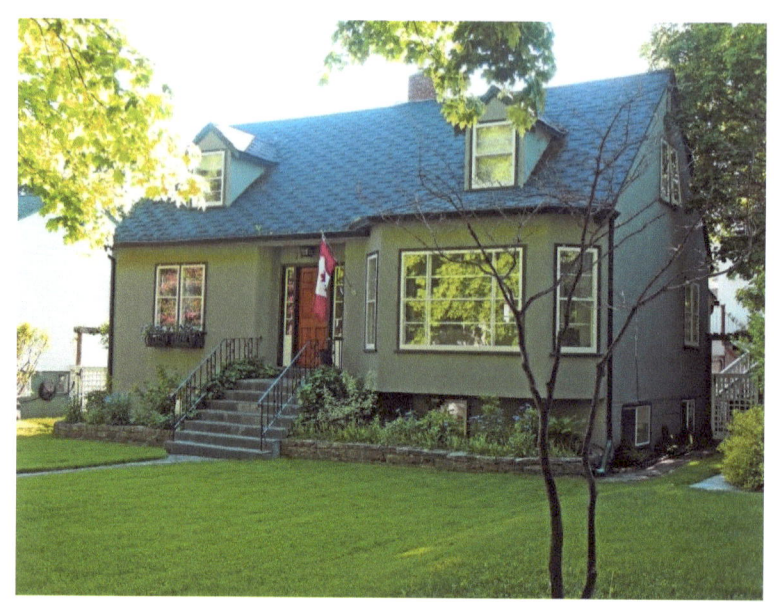

1870 Maple Street

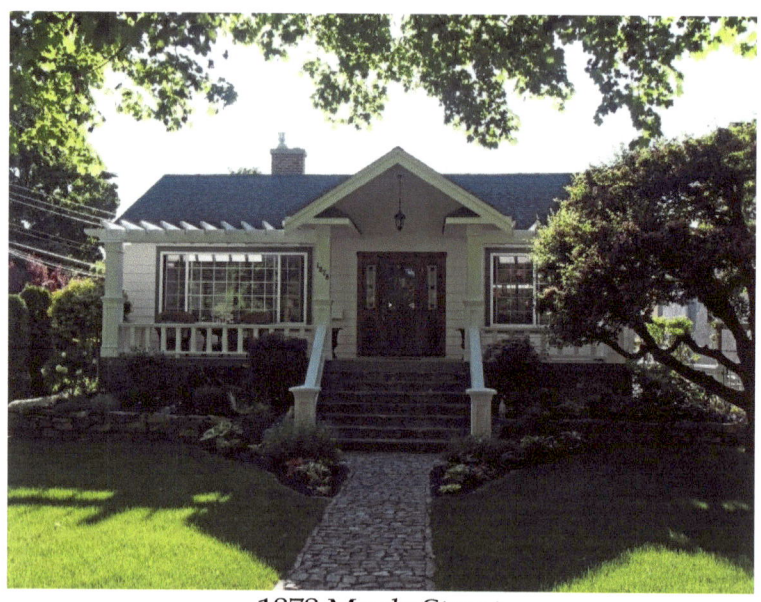

1878 Maple Street

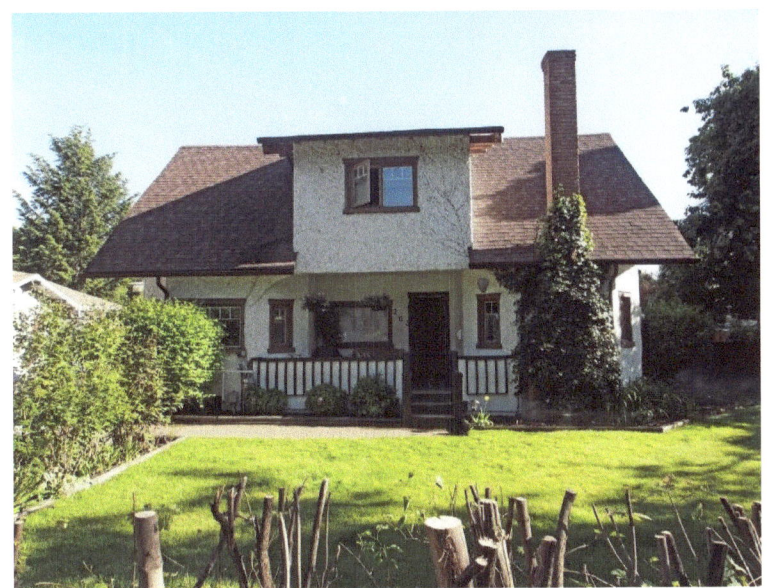

263 Lake Avenue

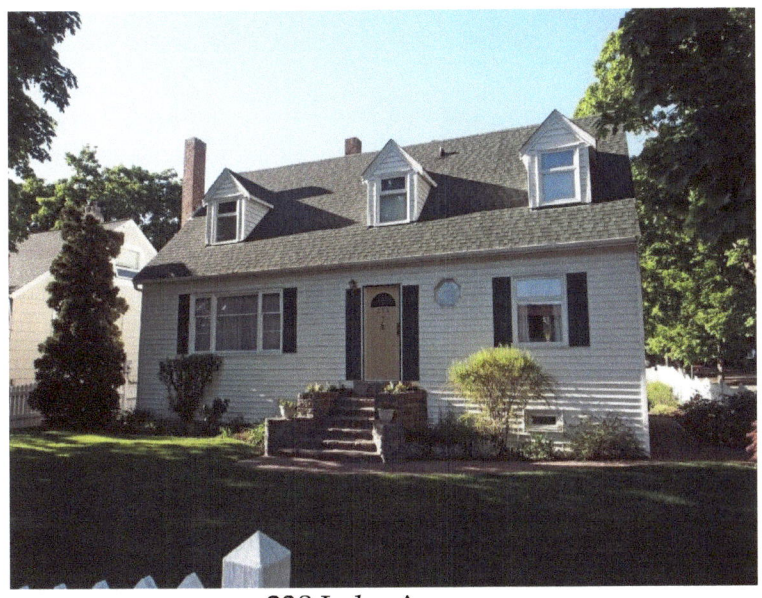

238 Lake Avenue

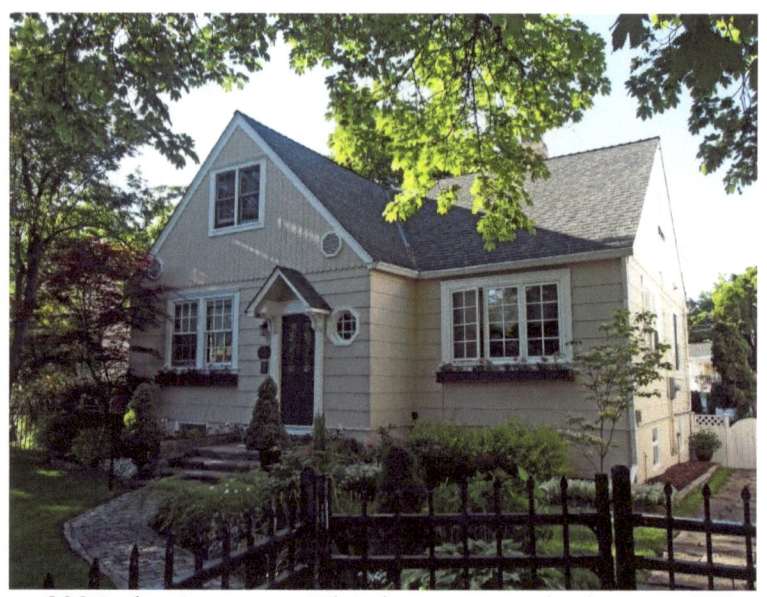

228 Lake Avenue – This house was the home of Harold Pettman and his family. Harold and his brother Charles ran Pettman Brothers Grocery until 1966 when Harold became Manager of the Okanagan Federated Shippers. This 1½ storey wood frame house was built in 1941 during the wartime. It is in Cape Code style. It has a cross-gabled roof, and a concrete foundation. There is horizontal siding on the first storey and vertical siding with polygonal ends on the upper half-storey. A small gabled roof supported with brackets covers the front entrance.

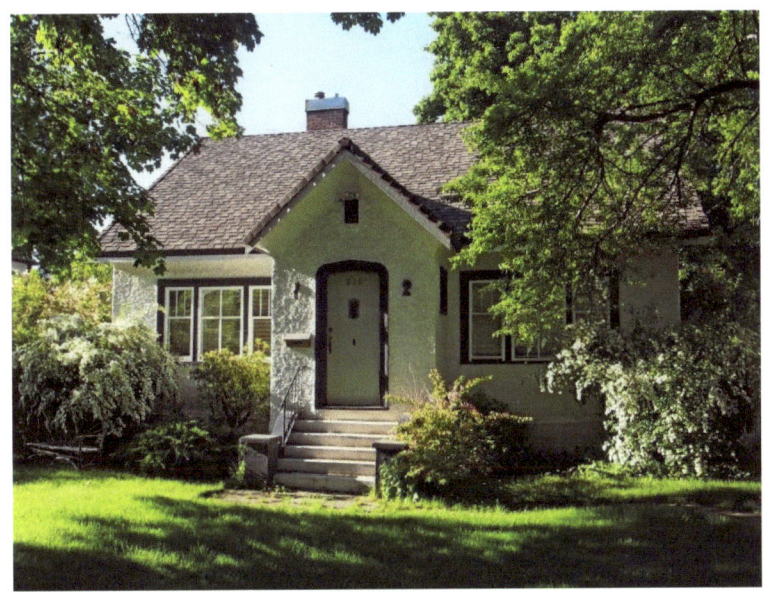

220 Lake Avenue

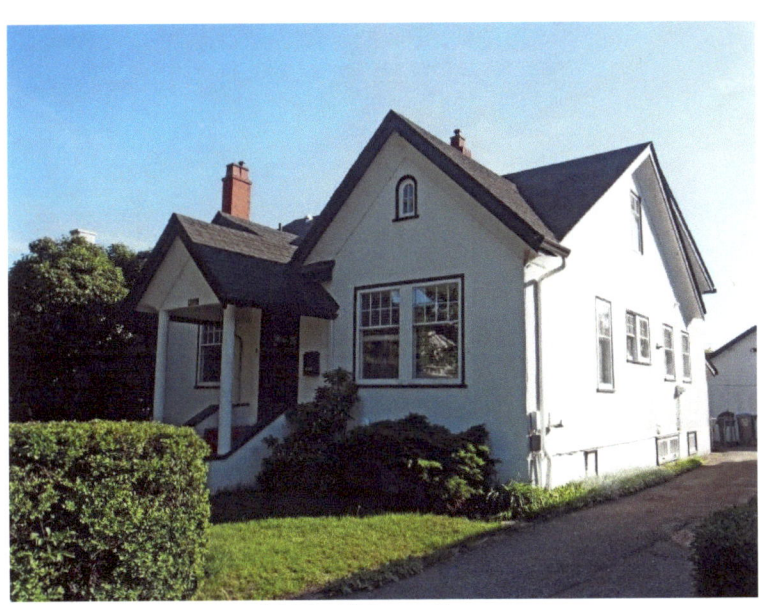

1908 Abbott Street

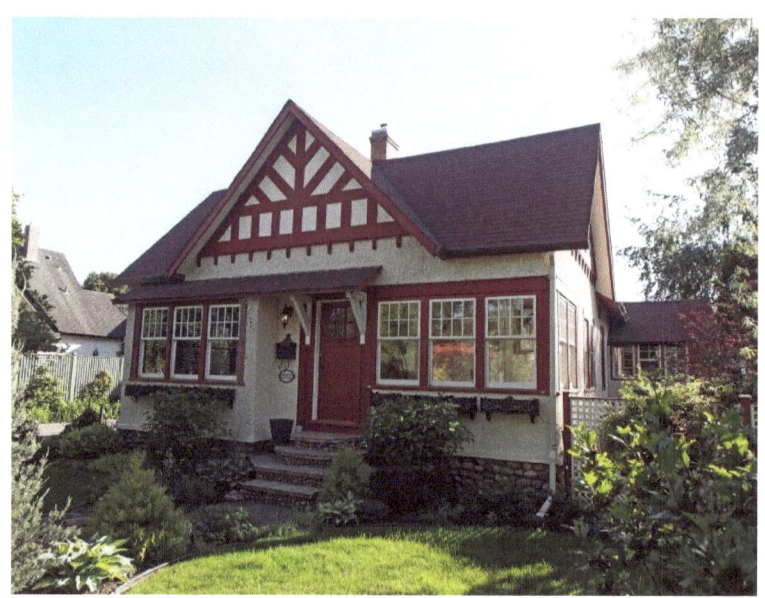

1912 Abbott Street – Tudor Revival style – decorative half-timbering, steeply pitched roof, prominent cross gables, tall narrow windows with small panes

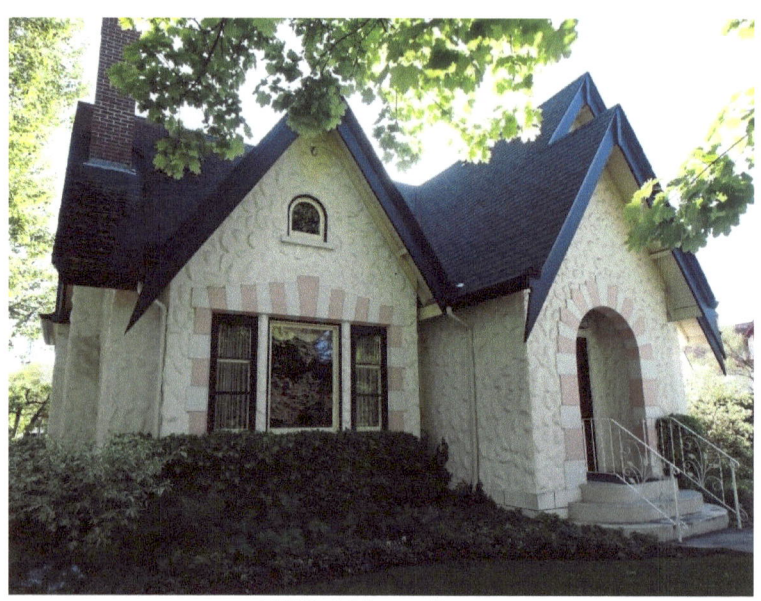

1922 Abbott Street

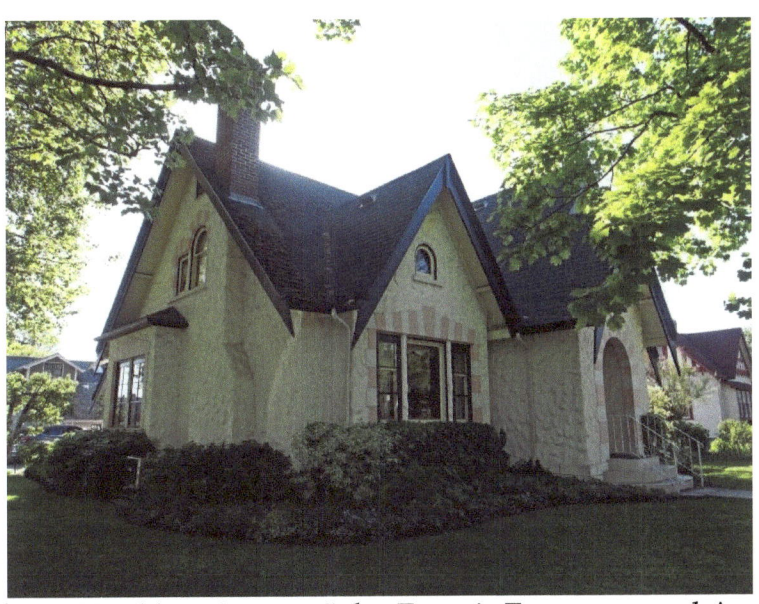

1922 Abbott Street – John Francis Fumerton and Annie Maria brought their family to Kelowna in 1916 where he established a men's clothing, dry goods and shoe store. This 1½ storey wood frame house was built in 1933 on the corner of Abbott and Vimy. With its picturesque roofline and casement windows, this Storybook cottage is a romantic representation of traditional domestic ideals. It has a steeply-pitched cross-gabled roof with gabled projections, its original glazed front door and semi-circular concrete front entrance steps.

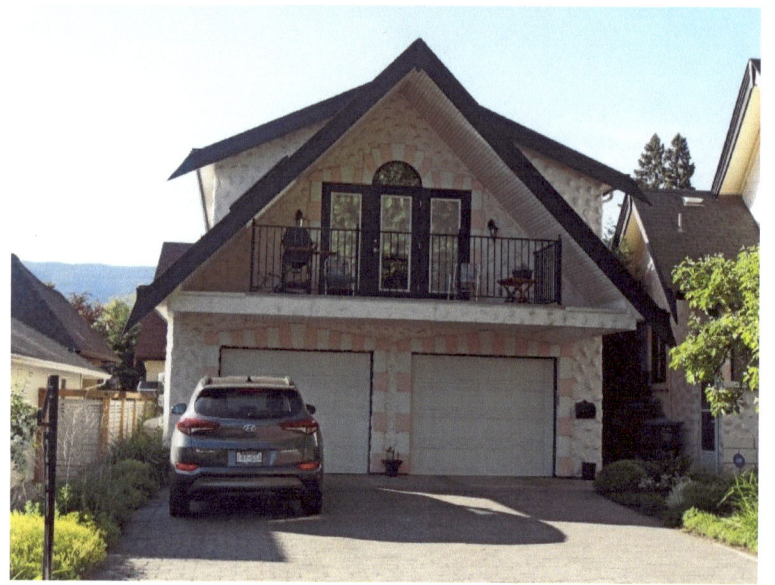

248 Vimy Avenue

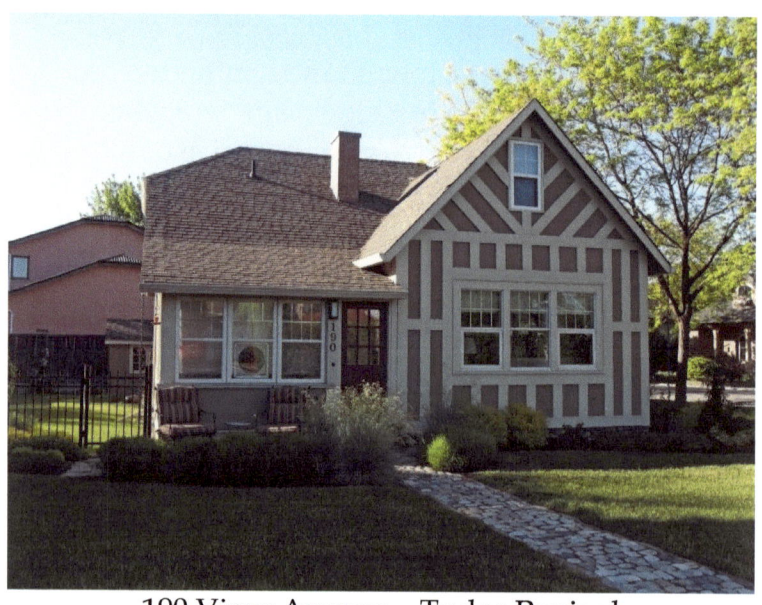

190 Vimy Avenue – Tudor Revival

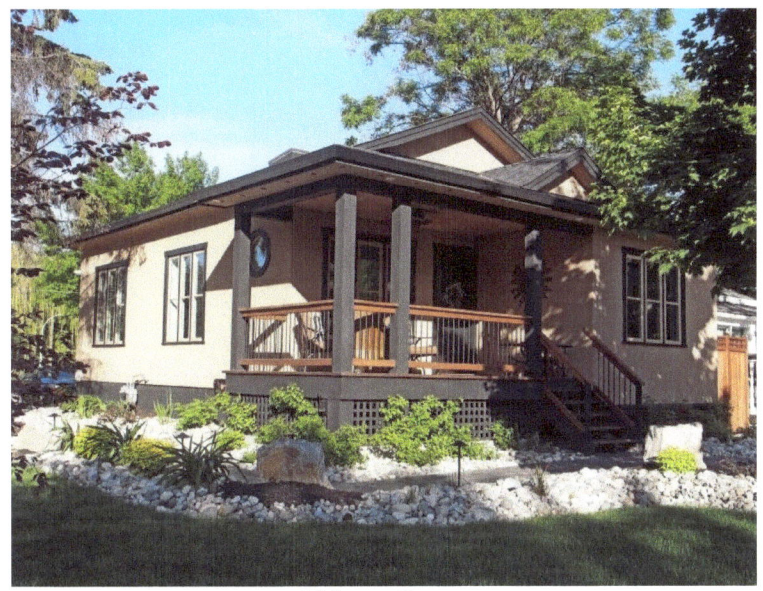

Abbott Street

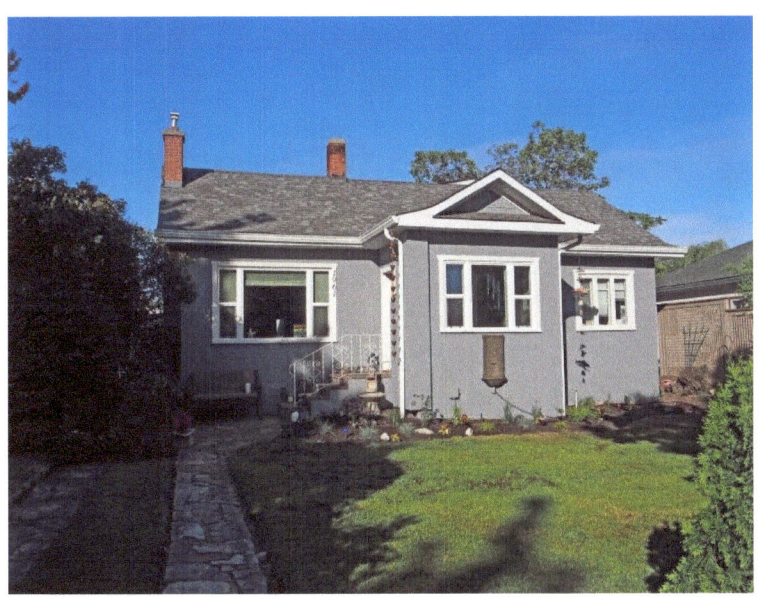

1961 Abbott Street

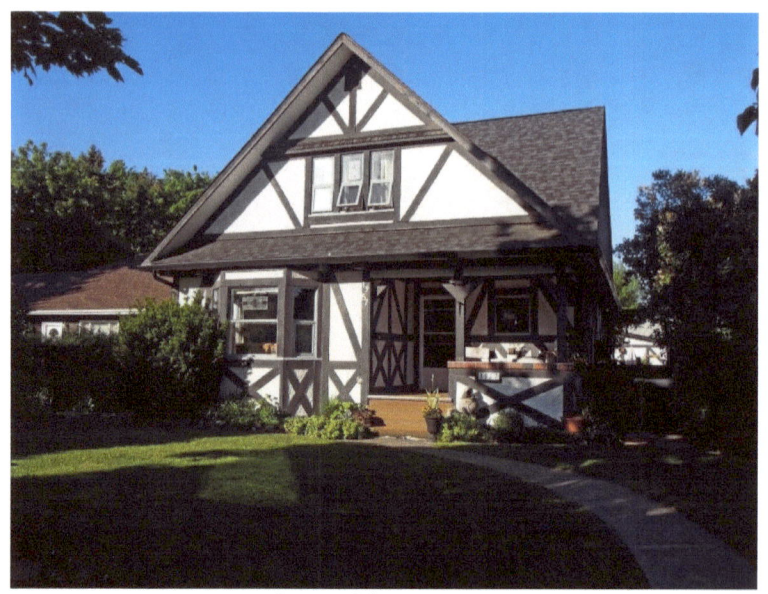

1957 Abbott Street

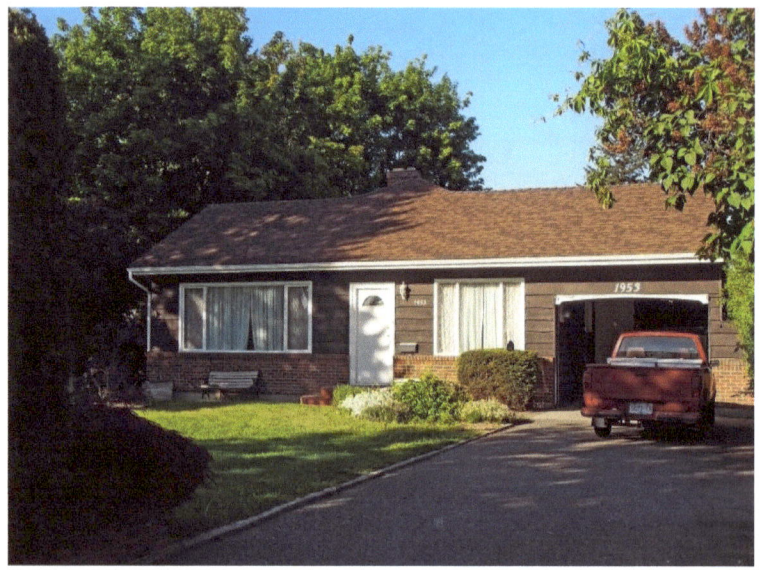

1953 Abbott Street

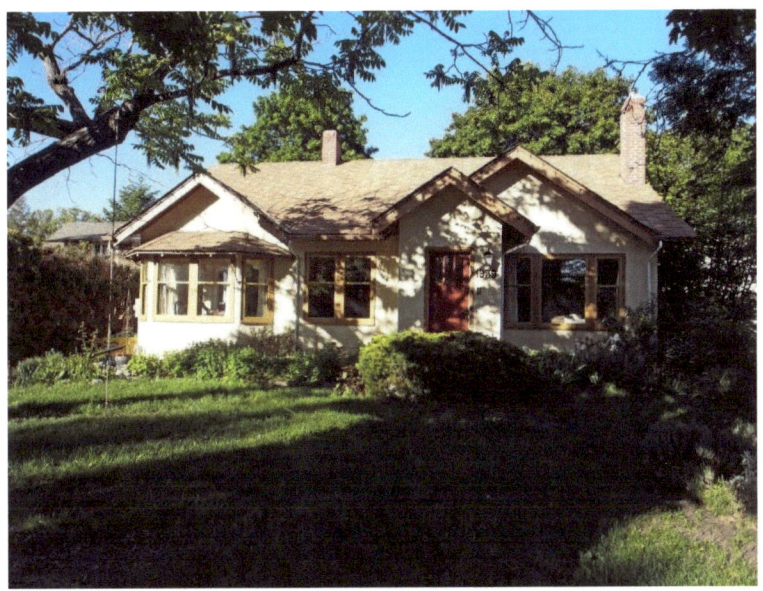

1939 Abbott Street

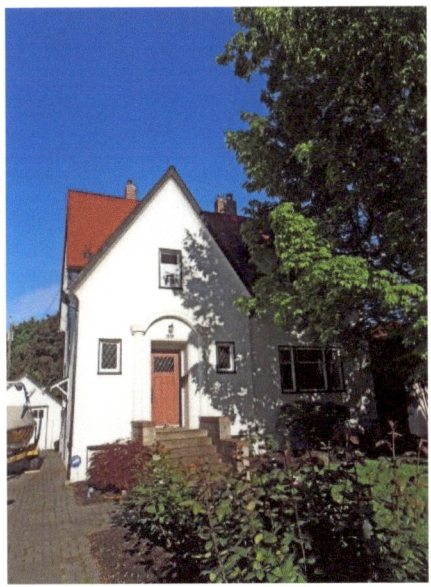

1853 Abbott Street – The Vernacular Cottage, built in the 1930s for Frederick Joseph and Annie Marcia Willis, has a steeply pitched gable roof. It has rounded pedestals at the entrance. He was Manager of the Kelowna Branch of the Royal Bank of Canada.

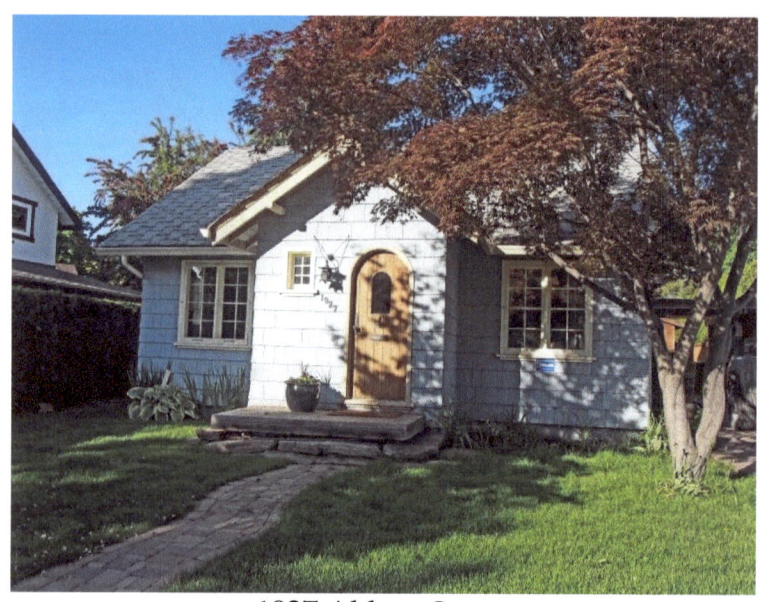

1927 Abbott Street

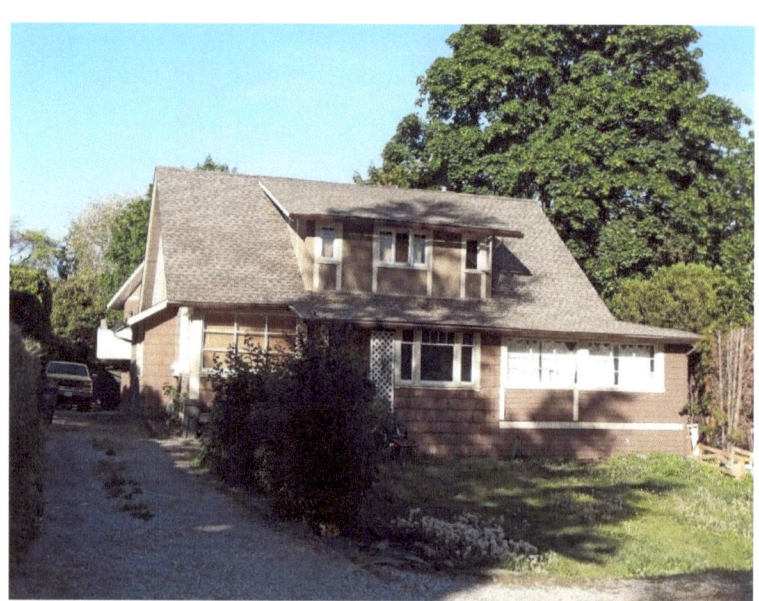

Abbott Street

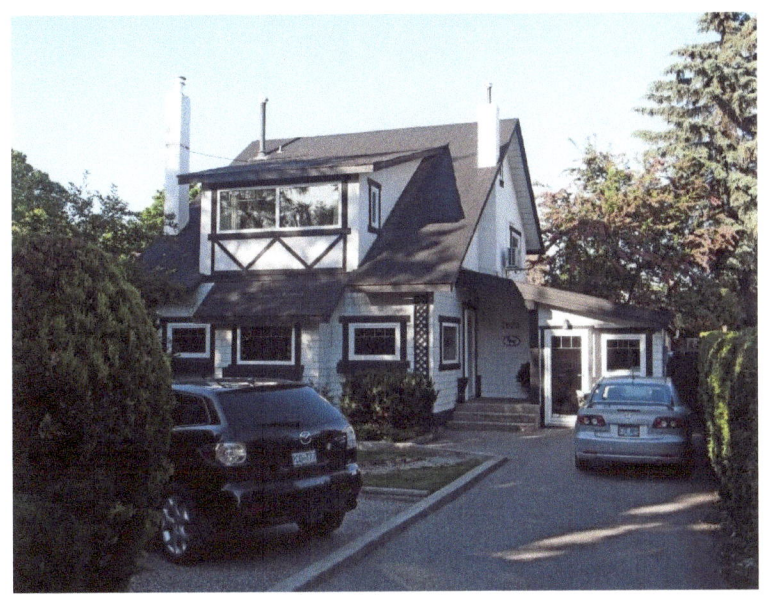

1923 Abbott Street

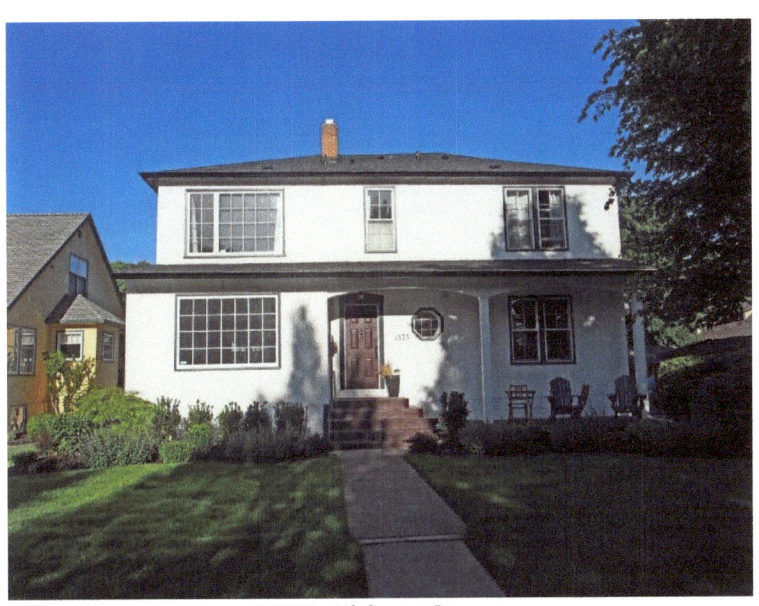

1875 Abbott Street

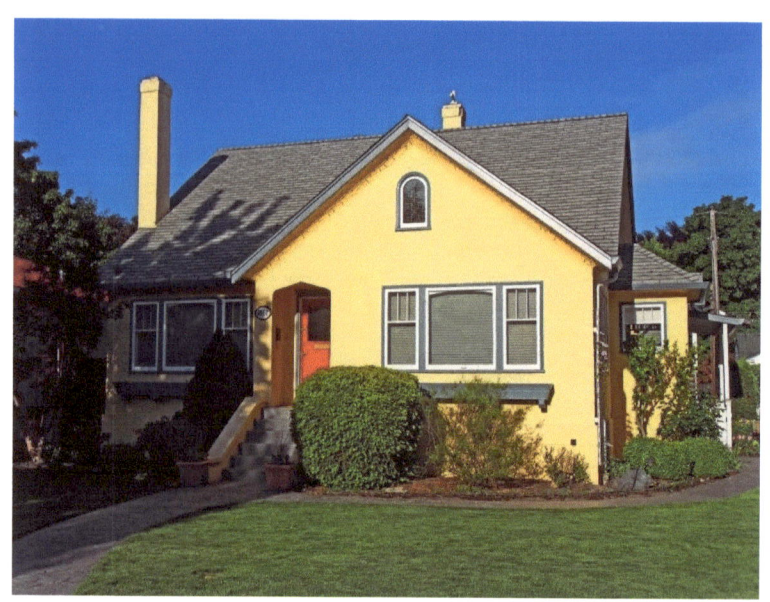

1867 Abbott Street

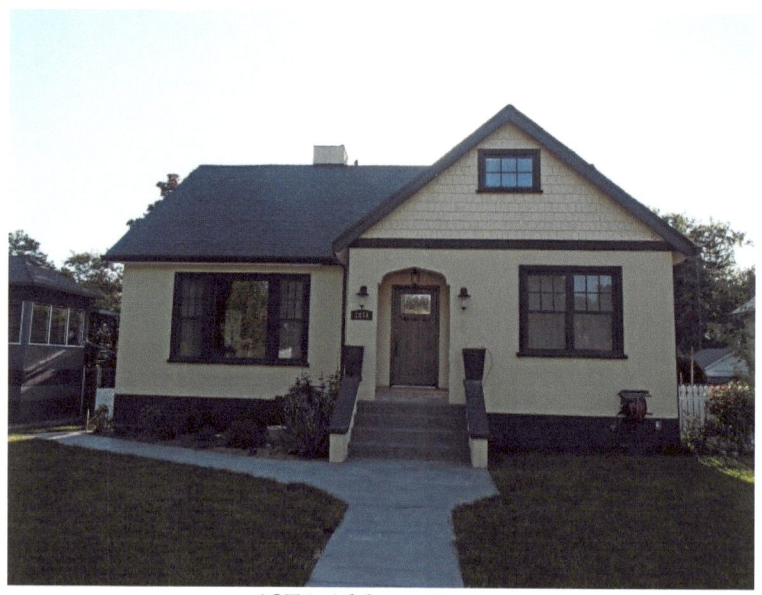

1874 Abbott Street

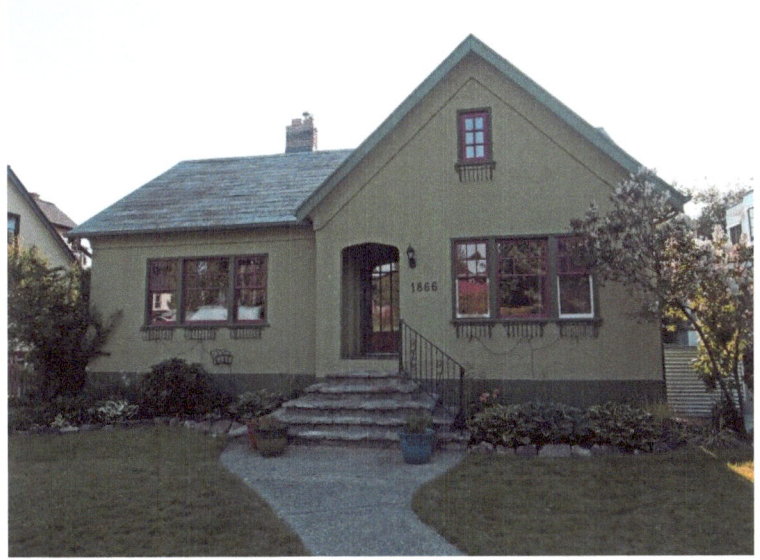

1866 Abbott Street

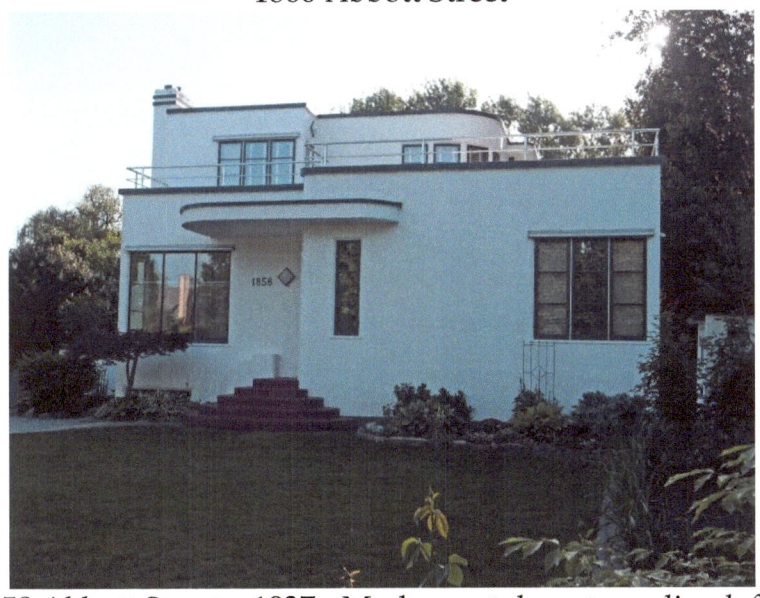

1858 Abbott Street – 1937 - Moderne style – streamlined, flat parapet roof, stucco and horizontal banding and cladding, multi-sash windows with narrow trim, curved walls, asymmetrical façade, canopy over entrance

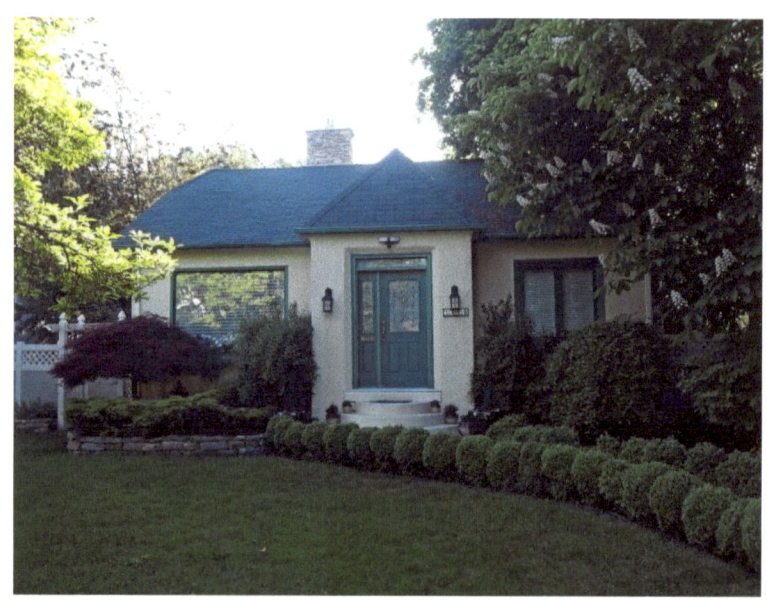

1850 Abbott Street – This vernacular cottage home was built between the first and second world wars (circa 1930). It reflects a simple and straightforward design of horizontal emphasis with a low gable shingled roof and a steeper roofed entry vestibule. The Parkinson family came to Kelowna in 1906. Dick Parkinson was involved in the fruit industry of the Okanagan and opened fruit wholesale houses in Calgary, Regina and Saskatoon. Dick loved sports and lobbied for parks and sports fields. In 1939, at the age of 38, he became the youngest member of City Council. He was known as "Mr. Regatta" for his support of this annual event on Lake Okanagan. After serving in World War II, he was again elected to City Council in 1948; he held this position until 1958 when he became Mayor of Kelowna (he served until 1969).

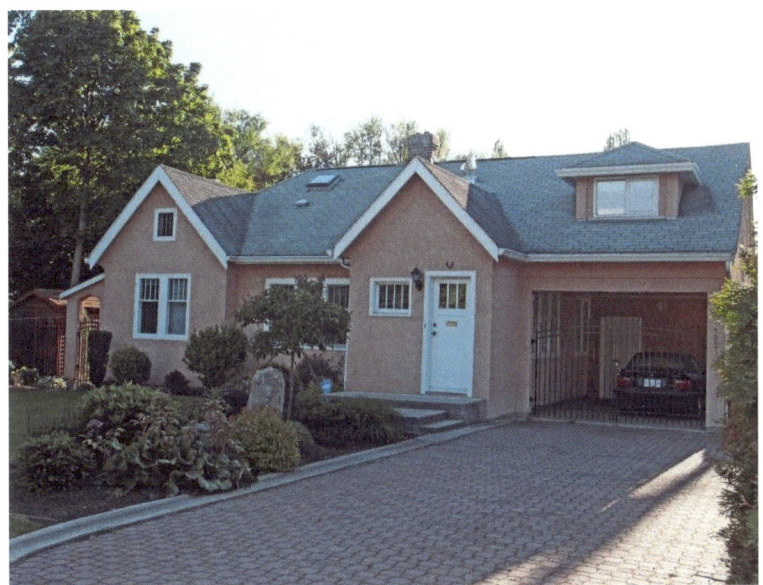

1826 Abbott Street

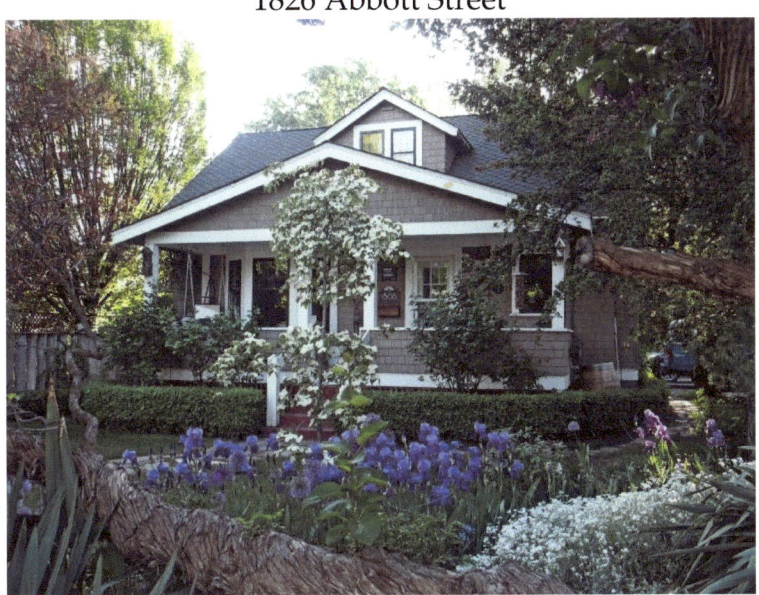

1806 Abbott Street – 1922 – stone house - Arts & Crafts style – exposed natural materials, low-pitched gable roof with wide, unenclosed eave overhand, roof rafters exposed, decorative beams and braces, porch supports extending to ground level

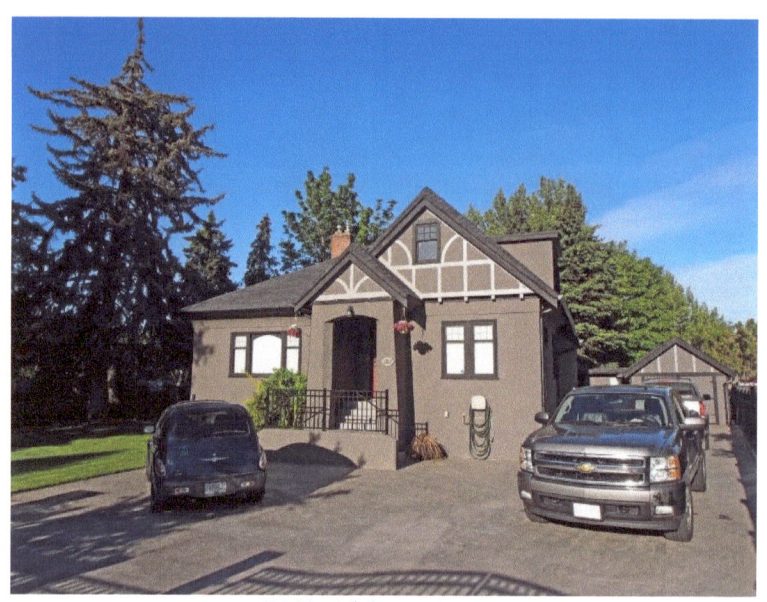

1763 Abbott Street

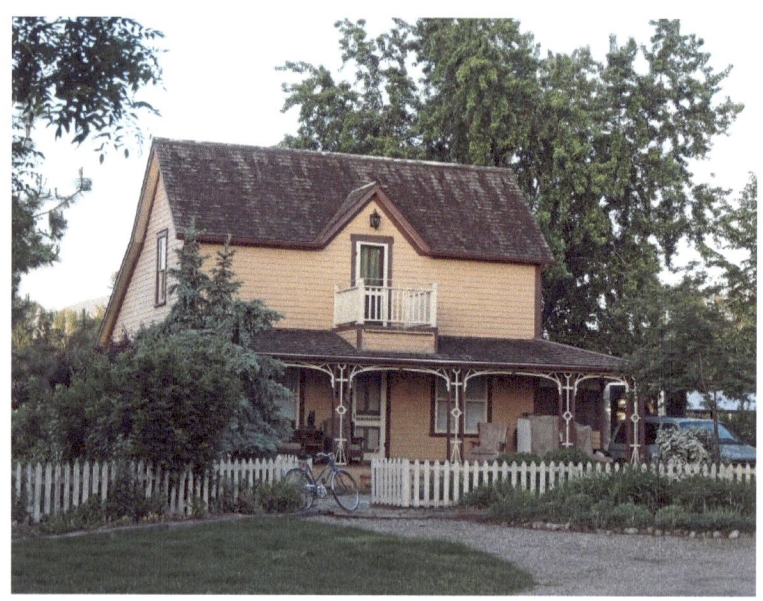

Abbott Street

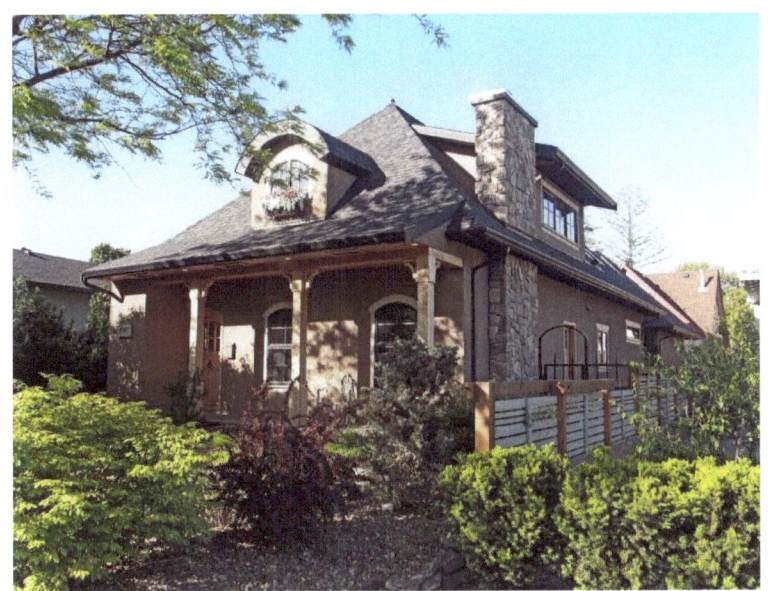

1945 McDougall Street

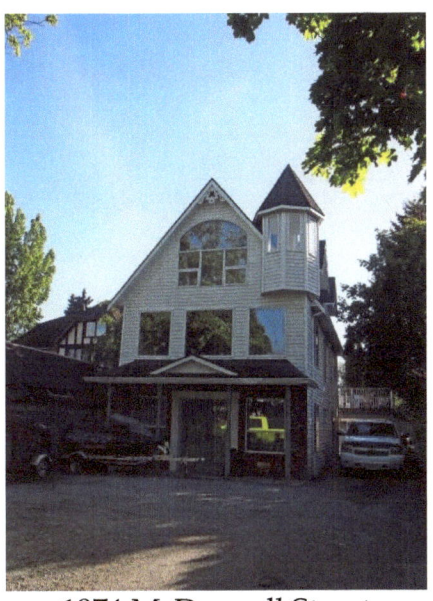

1974 McDougall Street

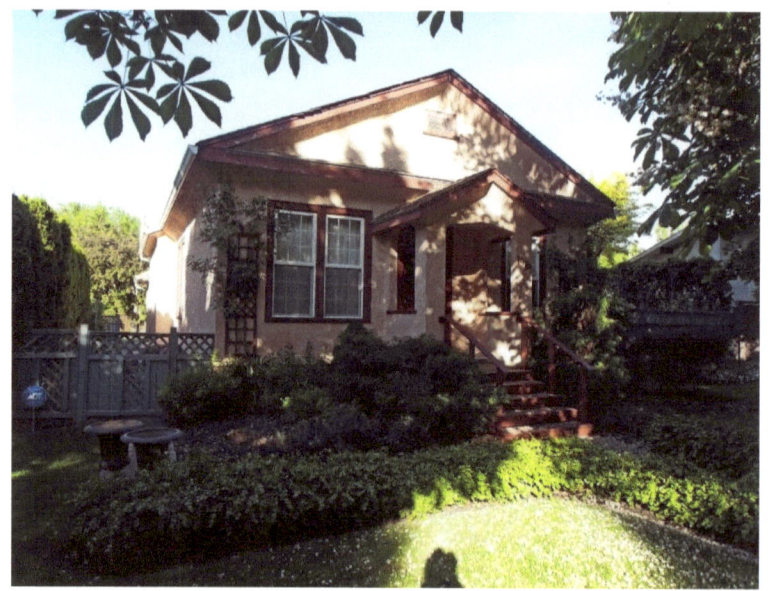

1989 McDougall Street

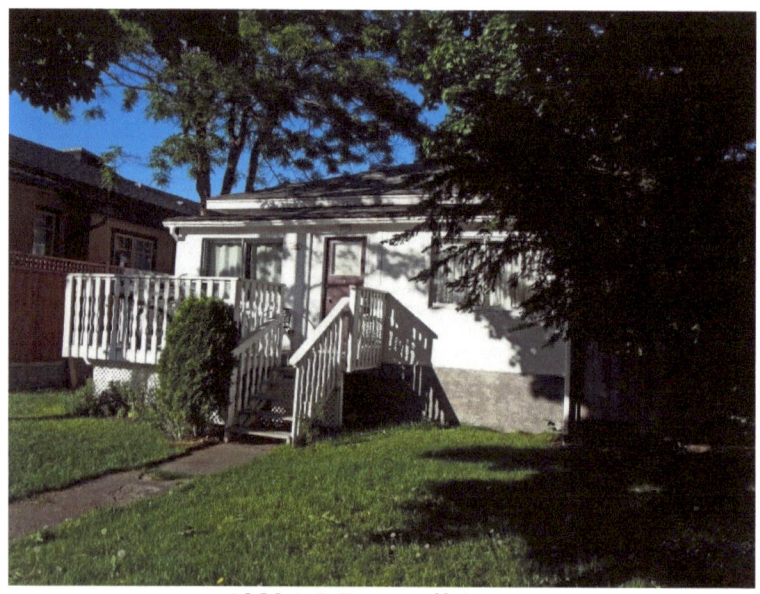

1983 McDougall Street

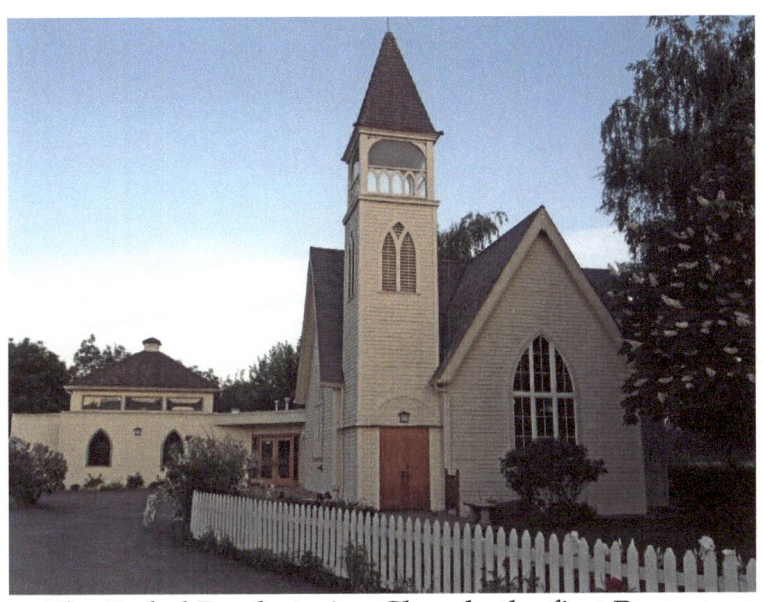

The Bethel Presbyterian Church, the first Protestant Church built between Vernon and the U.S. border, was built in 1892. The wood-framed and sided building is Gothic Revival in design with its steep cross-gabled roofs, cruciform plan, prominent bell tower and pointed-arched windows. It closed as a church in 1964. The Central Okanagan Heritage Society restored the building between 1982 and 1986 and it reopened as Benvoulin Heritage Church.

www.ingramcontent.com/pod-product-compliance
Lightning Source LLC
Chambersburg PA
CBHW040230220526

45473CB00001B/189